LAKELAND
REPORTER

LAKELAND REPORTER

RECOLLECTIONS OF A CUMBRIAN NEWSPAPERMAN

JOHN HURST

CUMBERLAND AND WESTMORLAND HERALD
SUTTON PUBLISHING

First published in 1996 by
Sutton Publishing Limited • Phoenix Mill
Thrupp • Stroud • Gloucestershire • GL5 2BU

A catalogue record for this book is available from the British Library

ISBN 0-7509-1289-8

Cover pictures: *top:* Bluebird *at speed on Ullswater; bottom: dogs stream away at the
start of a hound trail, near Mungrisdale, between Penrith and Keswick.*

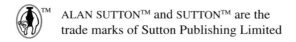 ALAN SUTTON™ and SUTTON™ are the
trade marks of Sutton Publishing Limited

Typeset in 11/12pt Erhardt
Typesetting and origination by
Sutton Publishing Limited
Printed in Great Britain by
WBC Limited, Bridgend.

Contents

Preface

'Write me a couple of sticks,' my first boss told me. Sticks! What was the man talking about? I was totally baffled.

As a newcomer to the wondrous world of newspapers, I soon found there was a great deal more I didn't know about. The learning process was to last for years because in 1945 there were a great many mystifying facets to news publication, even at what was perceived to be the lowest level, the weekly paper – the basic techniques of reporting, editing, proof reading, sports reporting, book reviewing, drama criticism, feature writing and the exacting task of local government coverage. On national daily papers there are specialists in most of these aspects but, over fifty years ago, anybody joining a weekly publication like the Penrith-based *Cumberland and Westmorland Herald* had to be prepared to tackle all the phases of journalistic work as part of a small team.

I soon learnt that the stick referred to by my first boss, Robert Irving, was a printer's stick for the composing of type by hand, no longer in common use in 1945, although the term still cropped up as a rough guide to the suggested length of reports.

There was much more for the raw novice to fathom, for the talk was of ems and ens, lower case and upper case, founts and formes, adds and follow-ups, proofs, revises and stets – just some of a vast glossary of strange terms seldom heard outside newspaper offices and printing works.

Old times vanish. Advances in technology, along with college courses for budding journalists, have brought about immeasurable improvements in news publications, but no computer could ever replace the old-style newshounds. They were rather special men and women who were often seen as wasting time in idle conversation when, in fact, they made major contributions to newsgathering by picking up offbeat stories and more besides. Mixing with people and developing contacts were – and still are – essential to the success of a newsman or woman. If they also have computer skills, so much the better.

There was a great deal more to reporting than chasing up stories of drama, excitement and humour. The detailed coverage of outdoor events, such as agricultural shows, could be exacting and tiresome, but there was ample consolation. Although many reporting missions demanded intense concentration, they were made endurable by the fact that we worked in radiant countryside – the lush expanse of the Eden Valley of Cumbria, fringed to the east by the Pennines and to the west by the Lake District mountains, an area of idyllic villages and scenic delights.

This book is intended to recall the range of work and experience of a country reporter in what I think of as vanished times, long before the brave new world of computerization and time-saving devices. In the setting up of type, the stick's successor was the Linotype machine, which has also passed into oblivion as I write this. So has the humble typewriter as the principal means of writing news copy, and the pedal cycle as a vehicle for chasing up news stories and following fire engines. Yes, the pushbike has disappeared, apart from the frame of a former colleague's sit-up-and-beg model which now gathers dust in a store room.

Men have also passed into the sphere of cherished memory. Robert Irving, Robert Burne and Tom Sarginson are all unforgettable to me because they were THE men of the *Herald* in the forties and fifties, helped me through my early fumblings as a reporter and instilled in me some of the romance of the profession. Their advice and guidance, plus occasional angry shouts of remonstration, were an indelible influence.

Long-service journalist and mentor of young reporters Robert Irving (right) was also a leading football administrator and chairman of the now-defunct Penrith and District League. The footballers are Harry Garrity of Braithwaite FC (with cup) and Bill Coulthard of Threlkeld FC. This picture is from the late 1950s.

CHAPTER 1

Meeting my Mentor

The reporters' room and the printing works are at the very heart of a weekly newspaper, while the journalists and the printers make it beat or, just occasionally, miss a beat. Nowadays, they can call on computerized paraphernalia to ease the task of converting raw copy into eye-catching pages of print and pictures, but in 1945 there were no computers. In fact, there wasn't even a typewriter in the first reporters' room I worked in, and I was truly a scribe – though not exactly with a quill pen.

Nor was the *Herald* office of my youth manned by eager young men wearing green eyeshades or with ties slackened and hats jammed on the backs of their heads, as in the Hollywood movies. The building never echoed to cries of 'I've got a scoop' or 'Hold the front page'.

When I joined the staff in 1945 the Second World War was in its last months and the younger reporters were still in the forces. I found myself working alongside an editor aged over seventy, a sub-editor in his mid-sixties, a manager-cum-reporter in his forties and a part-time proof reader aged over sixty. I was sixteen and a half.

I was in awe of my first editor, Tom Sarginson, a legendary local figure, widely known by his pseudonym of 'Silverpen', who by then had been on the staff for over half a century. For most of that time he had written the keynote feature, 'Notes and Comments', originally a chatty column on the news of the week, which he honed with care and pride and turned into the editorial on reaching the top.

I was granted the honour of an interview with the great man late one Friday afternoon in the summer of 1944. The make-up of the paper, due out the next day, had by then been completed and there was time for lesser matters. I had nursed ambitions of becoming a reporter since I was a small boy when I read crime and sports reports in the newspapers in my grandmother's little shop and developed an interest in how the papers were put together – the daily or weekly miracle of writing and assembling the mass of information and pictures. I sustained my hopes by writing scraps for the school magazine and producing occasional copies of a street newspaper, all laboriously written by hand. My father paid two guineas to enable me to join a correspondence course with the London School of Journalism. Perhaps I could be a sports reporter and be paid for watching my favourite sports of cricket and football?

Tom Sarginson looked down on me as I occupied a low sofa-like chair in his

A man of influence and fine words. Tom Sarginson, better known as 'Silverpen', was the Herald's editor from 1913 until he died in 1951, at the age of 81. At the coronation of George VI in 1937 he was one of five weekly newspapermen invited to represent the provincial press. His account of the scene in Westminster Abbey was one of the finest pieces of descriptive writing about the historic occasion.

office. This was nearest thing I have known to being in the presence of God and, as the torrent of nervous words poured from me, I hoped that they made sense. Somehow I struggled through his questions and described how I would handle the reporting of a fire, the brief details of which he dictated to me.

Then, glory be, he offered me a job – £1 a week, nine to five (but be prepared to work some evenings each week), to begin at the start of 1945, after I had re-taken several subjects to improve a rather unimpressive School Certificate at Penrith Grammar School.

Elation soared at the realization of an ambition: I was a newspaperman. But Tom Sarginson sounded a warning note as I shook hands with him and prepared to leave. 'Perhaps I should mention,' he said, 'that George Hobley is in the RAF and Frank Shaw in the Army. They'll be back as soon as the war is over – so we might have to review the situation . . .'

Clearly, I must do my best to impress before Germany surrendered!

Then, as now, the advertisement office fronted onto King Street, which carried the A6 through the centre of the market town of Penrith, but printers and reporters worked in the nether regions. A thirty-yard passageway led to a rambling building which housed the Cossar flat-bed printing press on the ground floor. Immediately above were the reporters' room and, beyond that, an office shared by Tom Sarginson and manager Robert Burne, while on the top floor were the clanking Linotype machines, which converted news and advertisement copy into lead type, and the printing stone, over which men toiled and perspired as they performed the weekly jigsaw puzzle of making up the pages of articles, illustrations and advertisements, ready for the readers every Saturday morning.

On 2 January 1945, I walked down the passageway from King Street and climbed the well-worn wooden stairs to meet the most important man in my working life — my mentor, driving force and inspiration, sub-editor Robert Irving. A distinguished white-haired man, he sat at a big, flat-topped desk, whisking his way through the daily intake of news copy, mainly reports of auction marts, Women's Institute meetings, village events like parish councils, bring and buy sales, annual meetings, church and chapel services.

Robert's desk was heavily scarred with inkstains of many colours and with thousands of stab marks where he had driven in his pen-knife after sharpening his sub-editing pencil or peeling one of the small, rather sour apples which he brought from his garden. There were also masses of paper – some, like the news items, getting prompt attention, and others more permanent, such as pads of unused copypaper, council minutes and agendas, old newspapers, half-filled notebooks and some documents of uncertain vintage or purpose. So much paper pours into newspaper offices that it becomes the scourge of newsrooms, raising occasional fears that, unless urgent action is taken, the staff will be submerged by the stuff.

The village reports, which my new boss was handling, were generally short, uncomplicated and contained a lot of names of sports winners, stallholders, tea ladies and members of newly elected committees. Names are the very bedrock of papers like the *Herald*. 'Names are news,' I was told, 'but, for goodness sake, see that you spell them correctly.' However brilliant a piece of writing may be, it will be condemned and cast aside by at least one reader if a mistake is made in the spelling of a name.

Robert Irving corrected any errors of punctuation and chopped out excessive verbiage before writing headlines. These went to the printers on separate bits of coloured paper, to be set on a different Linotype machine from the reports. The two were linked together later by means of catchlines scribbled on the top of the news items.

The Linotype operators, Billy Parkin, Dick Dixon and Tommy Varty, set most of the articles in eight point type, but auction mart and WI reports were marked to be set in the smaller six point – a reduction made essential because newsprint was in short supply in wartime. Papers were down to eight pages or sometimes only six, and the more run-of-the-mill news had to be condensed as much as

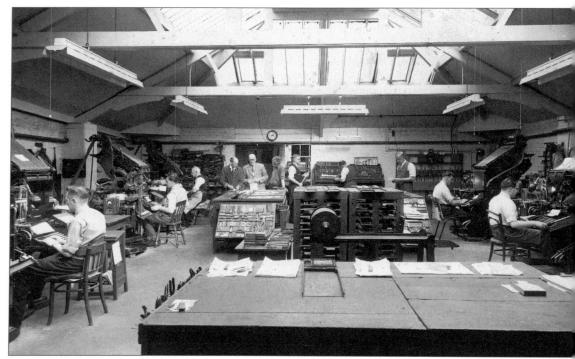

The days when newspaper type was set in hot lead by Linotype machines is recalled by this picture of the Herald *printing works in about 1960. Standing in the centre, studying a proof, is Robert E. Burne, who rose through the editorial ranks to become managing director.*

possible. (Even years later, with larger papers, six or seven point type was employed as a space-saver.)

My new boss broke away from his task to tell me something about office routine. My Monday morning jobs included filling in the office diary with brief details of any forthcoming events – annual meetings, bring and buy sales, flower shows, ploughing or turnip hoeing competitions, football matches, special sales at the auction marts, dog, rabbit or bird shows – all listed in the advertising columns in the previous week's paper. Agendas of local councils came in through the post to boost diary entries. Robert decided which of the engagements should be covered by reporters. A scribbled 'JH' told me that attendance of the annual meeting of the town's YMCA was to be my first journalistic job of any merit.

With the diary completed, there were the daily calls to be made – a check by telephone of police and fire stations, hoping to get word of any burglaries or blazes but frequently yielding only an abrupt 'Nowt' from the duty officer. If time permitted, the check calls were made by walking or cycling to the police station, a much more effective way of establishing contacts. Acquaintanceships developed as a teenage junior were to pay dividends many years on, for policemen tend to have long memories and remember the reporters who are keen to get a story.

'How's your shorthand?' inquired Robert Irving. It was a difficult and embarrassing question which he asked with some frequency in the early years. Isaac Pitman's brand of speed-writing was essential to anybody entering journalism but learning the skill could be long and demanding. I had taken night lessons at a small commercial school, while still attending the grammar school, but I could never match some of the star performers, with speeds of up to two hundred words a minute. Although Robert gave me occasional tests, hoping to boost my speed, it was never more than adequate.

'You had better do the "Looking Backwards",' I was instructed. The column was one of the most popular features of the paper, made up of extracts from the *Herald* of half a century before – nostalgic backward glances to the Victorian era, containing many quirky news items and enabling senior readers to recall old friends and achievements of yesteryear. In later years the flashback column was extended to cover twenty-five and a hundred years before, as the appetite for memorabilia grew.

I performed this duty with enthusiasm for many years and never found it a bore. There were plenty of piquant paragraphs and the exercise taught me a lot about the construction and vital elements of news stories, although the style was outdated. I now feel that my hours spent producing 'Looking Backwards' developed in me a love of research which, in later years, led to the writing of several local histories on the theme of sport.

Some will find it strange that the quietude of the reporters' room was never broken by the hammering of typewriters as I turned out my earliest copy, be it the Penrith YMCA annual meeting report or some other. The only typewriter was ensconced in the editor's room, although manager Robert Burne also used it occasionally. All my early contributions had to be written by hand on thick pads of copypaper, made up of sheets of unused newsprint from the reel ends, cut down to a suitable size and pasted together. Occasionally, the reverse sides of rejected hand-outs, council minutes and other unwanted documentation went into the pads. Nothing was wasted in the newspaper office of my teenage years.

We jammed the pads into our pockets when we left for courts and council meetings, so that, if a lull in the proceedings permitted, we could write up some of the stories on the spot, ready to be handed in as soon as we got back to the office. To speed up the writing of stories, we used dozens of contractions – w with, wt without, t the, tt that, sd said, ct court, ccl council, ctte committee, expln explanation, mtg meeting, ckt cricket, fbl football, gl goal and so on. A report might well begin, 'A wits at Pth Mags' Ct on Tues sd tt deft hd no expln . . .'.

The opportunities and challenges of my new job excited me. After all, I faced the prospect of meeting people in the limelight – well, the local limelight – as I chased up news stories and of being constantly at the hub of happenings upon the local scene, centred on Penrith but extending over the length of the Eden Valley and northern Lakeland, a truly delectable area to work in. There must be a catch, I thought, and, indeed, my sensation of self-satisfaction was soon to be severely dented. The reason: proofs!

The early stages of my career were dominated by the reading of proofs, a vital part of the production of newspapers but demanding, time-consuming and not the ideal form of occupation for an active teenager. Galley after galley of type was proofed onto strips of paper for checking against the original copy. My menial task was that of copy-holder, while my companion was Harry Harrison, a former editor of the rival paper, the *Penrith Observer*, who was then working as a freelance and spending a couple of days a week with the *Herald*. Harry had the more responsible job of perusing the proofs for omissions, transpositions and literals (misspellings).

Day after day, hour after hour, we sat on either side of the gas fire in the reporters' room, plodding our way through every word, comma, colon, full point, question mark and staggerer (exclamation mark) which were to appear on the following Saturday. Very occasionally I got a break from the toil, for one of the news stories under surveillance might bring back memories of Harry Harrison's earlier days in journalism and prompt him to tell a story or two. Because he was originally an *Observer* man, many of these anecdotes were at the *Herald*'s expense, such as that of the day, early in the thirties, when they were hours ahead of us in hearing about a murder and in getting to the scene, in a remote hamlet. Then there was the one about the embarrassing error, made by the *Herald*, of course, when the name of Appleby's Shire Hall was misspelt. Yes, you guessed it . . .

Perhaps Harry's favourite tale concerned a flower show in one of the villages where a Mr Chugg was the most successful competitor. In setting up the report, the *Herald* Linotype operator mischievously spaced out the lines so that, in glancing down the leading edge of the column, the reader saw:

Chugg,
Chugg,
Chugg,
Chugg,
Chugg,

and so on.

Sub-editor Irving would put up with only so much of this time-wasting chatter. 'Come on, Harry. Get on with it,' he would growl. 'You two are as loquacious as a couple of washerwomen.'

One of my most difficult jobs as a proof reader was to hold the copy for editor Tom Sarginson when he checked his editorials, or 'Notes and Comments'. The original articles had been typed, but so numerous were the second thoughts, and second thoughts about second thoughts, that each folio was a mystifying mass of crossings–out and spidery lines shooting out in all directions to circles of squiggly replacements and additions in minute writing. My editor could get quite testy if I seemed unduly hesitant in following the complexities of the copy.

By the time I joined the staff Tom Sarginson was working a shortened day, generally arriving around ten in the morning, after being driven to the office, and leaving for coffee and then lunch at the George Hotel by 11.30 or so. He seldom stayed in the office beyond four o'clock in the afternoon, but what many people did not realize was that his evenings at home were spent in writing his 'Notes and Comments', carefully crafted works of mature judgement and wide outlook, full of colour, humour and patriotism. He was an avid supporter of Winston Churchill in his wartime editorials.

The Women's Institute movement is very strong in rural Cumbria. There was an air of eager anticipation among members of Nenthead WI as they sat down for dinner at their seventeenth birthday party in 1968. On the menu were turkey and all the trimmings, ice cream, coffee, cheese and biscuits and slices of a celebratory cake.

Although engaged to be a reporter, with proof reading as a secondary occupation, I was also the editor's errand boy. I had to make frequent visits to a herbalist's shop to purchase herb tobacco, which Tom mixed with a more standard brand. He also required special shoes, made and repaired by Matt Rowe, a local cobbler with a little shop in Sandgate which I visited with some frequency. It was all part of the job in the late forties. Thankfully, amidst the proof reading and the running of errands, there was plenty of time to learn the skills of filling the columns of the newspaper. In fact, I was introduced to sub–editing at a very early age.

Initially, it was the subbing of small advertisements and public notices so that they were in line with the paper's style. Words had to be rearranged so that the adverts never began with the words 'wanted' or 'for sale', but with the name of the article being sought or on offer, and there was a set pattern for the placing of commas and semi–colons. The same applied to births, marriages and deaths and to public notices giving details of shows, dances and other events.

Much more challenging and satisfying was the subbing of the Women's Institute reports, which I first tackled when only a teenager. Here, too, there was a set style, one rule being the elimination of any mention of the singing of the WI

The temperance movement has worthy advocates in the Vale of Eden Band of Hope Union which used to hold an annual 'demonstration', which alternated between the towns of Appleby and Kirkby Stephen – where this picture was taken in the 1960s. A parade of banners was followed by picnic meals, sports, football competitions, a Punch and Judy show and similar attractions, not forgetting temperance addresses.

anthem 'Jerusalem'. As it was sung at every meeting, it was hardly newsy, I was told. WI reports featured details of talks, social half-hours and tasty suppers (and all the names of the women who prepared and served them), but I was especially fascinated by the vast range of competitions. Some of them demanded considerable imagination, such as 'something new out of something old', most items in a matchbox and the 'best article made out of discarded black-out material', but pride and place must go to the ladies of Caldbeck who, in 1945, were asked to create something useful out of a flour bag. The powers of ingenuity and skill were such that they produced children's dresses, pinafores, a night-dress case and even a pair of cami-knickers!

Penrith teenagers twice set records in marathon jiving in 1960. The original record of twenty-seven hours was broken within a day. The youngsters then returned to the Drill Hall a month later and seven of them jived for forty hours, with three-and-a-half minute breaks every hour for food, drink and massage.

CHAPTER 2

Lots in a Name

People love to see their own names in the newspaper, preferably in a favourable context. Wherever I went, whatever the nature of the event, one of the main objects of the exercise was the accumulating of names. Village flower shows, for example, produced a rich crop in the form of firsts, seconds and thirds in classes for roses, dahlias and pot plants, cabbages, cucumbers, carrots and collections of vegetables. Recording them was a task of toil, sweat and concentration – there was no other way.

Judges' books containing results had to be collected and the details dictated to a colleague using a typewriter (yes, we had one by then!). Simple enough, you may think, but after we had churned out the successes of flower show exhibitors and still faced lists from vegetable, cookery and handicraft sections, plus the children's classes, tempers could become frayed and energy could wane. In my tenderfoot days the endeavour was not eased by the fact that, as we hammered out the winners' names in the corner of a village hall or a sweat-provoking marquee, we became a popular sideshow for gaping children and watchful busybodies.

'Potatoes (long) – first J. Smith, second C. Jones, third P. Brown,' droned the dictating reporter to his colleague, pausing for the detail to be typed out.

'No, that's not right,' a busybody interrupted. 'My dad won that class.'

'Well, that's what the results book says . . .'

'Then the book's got it wrong. My dad definitely won . . .'

So a time-consuming check had to be made of the individual result cards placed alongside the neat lines of potatoes on nearby trestle tables. It emerged that the book was perfectly correct. Dad had won – but for potatoes (round) – a different class altogether!

Just once was one of the interrupters welcomed. At one village show, the organizers saved on cash by using the same results books, year after year. My companion opened a book at page one and dictated thirty or so classes from an earlier year before the error came to light. But for an insistent busybody, we could have carried a full set of results from the show of two years before.

With results safely typed up, the reporter must turn to his introduction or 'intro', a more general look at the event, calling for a chat with the organizing secretary about entry numbers and a quote from the president on the standard of flowers and veg. It was amazing how many shows were the 'best ever'.

Hours spent at work in the countryside increased markedly as winter gave way to spring, bringing a host of sunlit events to test the descriptive powers, such as traditional May days on the Eden Valley village greens of Melmerby and Langwathby. The canny folk of Lazonby adopted a more cautious attitude and held their festivals inside the village hall at a time of year of uncertain weather. Curiously, none of the three villages had permanent Maypoles, whereas Temple Sowerby and Milburn boasted impressive poles but did not celebrate the month of May.

My first visit to Melmerby, at the foot of the Cumbrian Pennines, was with William Tunley, an elderly Penrith photographer. The Ribble bus took us only as far as the neighbouring village of Gamblesby, due to wartime restrictions, and I helped my companion to carry his old-style camera and tripod as we trudged along the 1½-mile road to Melmerby.

Two musicians, one playing an accordion and the other beating a drum, led the little procession. The May queen, seated side-saddle on a pony, was followed by page boys and ladies-in-waiting and the rest of the village children, some in fancy dress, and paraded round the green. A floral crown was placed on the queen's head in a short ceremony, on a platform set up under a burgeoning elm, and a 'royal proclamation' was read, calling for kindness to wildlife, dogs and cats.

There followed dancing on the green, sports for the children, a tea break, races and, possibly, a football match involving the older men and women of the village and a dance at night. The basic format did not alter much in the years following,

Melmerby May Day, on the village green at the foot of the Pennines, is one of East Cumbria's most colourful festivals. This picture was taken in 1968 when fifteen-year-old Sheilagh Teasdale was crowned Queen of the May. Her 'royal proclamation' urged children to be kind to birds and animals and to keep the village free from litter.

except that in some villages the fancy dress element became more striking through the creation of lavish and humorous tableaux, some on wagons or trailers drawn by farm tractors.

Further up the Eden Valley, at Musgrave and Warcop, the summer-time spectaculars to be reported were the rushbearings – re-enactments of the days, long ago, when peasants carried rushes to the parish churches to renew the floor coverings. Traditionally, boys carried crosses of rushes and girls wore floral crowns, in a parade to church, which, in the case of Warcop, was always accompanied by a top military band. Such musicians would normally cost hundreds of pounds but Warcop could call on them because the Army used nearby land as a tank-firing range, and, as Lords of the Manor, provided free lemonade and cakes for the children, as well as the swish band.

Garden parties, bring and buy sales and village fêtes were all part of the routine of the junior reporter. Every community had an annual 'do' and, although our correspondents covered many of them, I was despatched whenever possible, generally on my bike.

Robert Irving told me to pay special attention to the opening ceremony and, in particular, to the opening speaker, from whom words of great wisdom, even earth-shattering revelations, were seemingly expected. My experience was that these worthy ladies – men were seldom selected – generally fell into one of four categories: The weather-conscious ('I'm so sorry that I couldn't bring some

The fells at the head of Ullswater made a spectacular setting for Patterdale May Day in the 1950s. Similar events have been held for many years on the village greens at Melmerby and Langwathby.

sunshine with me' or 'I'm so glad we have such a glorious day'); the pleading ('This is such a good cause that I know you will all open your purses and handbags and clear the stalls'); the socially better-than-they-are ('We must do all we can to help our sisters who have fallen by the wayside'); and the nervous who used a minimum of words ('You didn't come here to listen to me so, without further ado, I will declare the garden party open').

Ritual demanded that, however brief or garrulous, thanks must be accorded to the speaker and the proposal was both moved and seconded in many cases. Then, before the ranks of spectators could disperse and descend upon the stalls, a small child emerged hesitantly from the throng, sometimes led by a proud mum, carrying a bouquet, a pot plant or some other gift for the opener.

Not a name must be missed as the reporter went the rounds of the stalls and sideshows, notebook at the ready. The tea ladies must be included and then there were the gate stewards and the harassed dogsbodies who did not have a specific task yet seemed to work harder than the rest, chasing about endlessly. A well-known figure, always willing to tell customers of what the future held in store, was Madame Yelmahc (the fortune teller's name in reverse).

Patrons listen attentively during a Penrith garden party, similar to the many that the newspaper used to cover. The opening ceremony is in progress and Herald *reporter Frazer Lindsay, with notebook at the ready, awaits the main speech.*

Hand in hand, schoolgirls walk through the Eden Valley village of Warcop, wearing floral crowns, followed by boys carrying crosses of rushes. The pretty festival marks the occasion of the annual rushbearing. The picture was taken in 1965 – although it could be from any year!

I never aspired to be a drama critic but in my early years in journalism many nights were devoted to watching amateur performances on local stages. As they were amateurs, there could be no hissing scorn or condemnation in what I wrote. The Penrith Players won many accolades for their plays but I must confess to a personal preference for the shows in village halls. Skills were probably lower but the atmosphere was one of countryfolk out to enjoy themselves and prepared to accept any shortcomings as inevitable.

A cherry-complexioned young farmer took the part of a debonair 'Who's for tennis?' type in one play I saw in a village in the Eden Valley. In one scene he had to light the cigarette of a demure young maiden, but the petrol lighter simply would not respond to repeated attempts. The audience watched in mounting agony as he flicked determinedly with a tiring thumb, until a voice boomed out from the back of the hall: 'Better git thisel a match, Bill, or we're ganna be here till bedtime.'

Dances, the other popular form of evening entertainment before television took over, also provided news copy or pictures. In the case of Saturday night 'bob hops' in the Drill Hall at Penrith, rowdiness sometimes occurred and men of violence appeared before the town magistrates, a few weeks later, while village dances were sometimes reported because beauty queens or show princesses were selected from among the dancers, or top bands played. Agricultural shows were often followed by crowded dances in boarded and illuminated marquees, at two shillings a head.

Amateur drama is popular in many Cumbrian towns and villages. Alston Players presented the comedy-thriller, Isn't life dull, *in 1961. Seated (left to right) are Campbell Burra, Muriel Thompson, John Sharratt, John Garbutt, Sylvia Cousin. Standing; Mamie Birkett, Joan Walton, Cynthia Harrison, Ethel Carr.*

Prizes were given for waltzing competitions, spot dances and obstacle dances, one of which I remember vividly after more than forty years. My partner, a well-built woman, the wife of a local farmer, was required to wear my jacket, turned inside out, as we foxtrotted. The encumbrances on me included keeping a balloon between my knees and – by way of a further challenge – the farmer's wife stood on my feet, with her shoes removed, and clung on for grim death as I inched across the dance floor. This was a considerable test of skill and stamina but we survived longer than the rest of the couples to win a packet of cigarettes each. This seemed a poor reward for the energy we had expended, especially as we were non-smokers.

News is not always readily identifiable; there are no helpful labels saying 'Write about this because it will fascinate the readers'. A story may get into the headlines because a reporter hears of an item with news potential during a casual conversation in the street, in a shop or in a restaurant, and realizes, from local knowledge, that what he has heard can be developed into an article which will demand attention. Journalists are not mere recorders of meetings and speeches;

Happy dancers in the Drill Hall at Penrith in 1953. This event was on Coronation Day but every Saturday evening saw a 'bob hop' in the hall, to the strains of Frank Walton and his Melody Makers. The town suffered a great loss when the hall was demolished after a fire in the early 1960s.

they must be able to spot a story in unlikely places, follow up and check. A front page feature may be the result of a coffee bar chat and a newspaperman's astuteness.

In my earliest days at the *Herald*, Friday afternoon saw the climax of the week's work – the build-up of news gathering, sub editing, collating of advertisements, setting of lead type and proof reading. Columns of type, headlines, picture blocks and adverts were finally assembled and locked into the frame-like formes by foreman Bert Winskill. From the composing room, on the top floor, they were lowered to the press, at ground floor level, and the final act commenced as the printing machine roared into action, the reels of newsprint revolved and the finished papers emerged. The weekly miracle was not quite complete, for the newly printed papers had then to be packed into bundles for local newsagents in towns and villages, or wrapped individually, ready for posting to ex-Cumbrians living, not only in many parts of Great Britain, but all over the world.

One of the joys of my early days at the *Herald* was, quite simply, to see my work in print. There was a unique intoxication in the transformation of a hand-written

Onlookers used the ruined remains of Penrith Castle to get a good view of the fancy dress competitors in the town's British Legion carnival as they walked along Ullswater Road, on their way to the football field, in about 1960.

report into a column of type, under an apt headline. Even more heartwarming was the merest murmur of praise or approval from a senior colleague. I cannot overstate my belief in my first editor, sub-editor and manager. They were heroic figures to me – the men who had set the style and created the character of the paper. All three spent over half-a-century with the *Herald* and in the case of Robert Irving the years totalled seventy-two when his time as a director was added to his half-century of reporting and editing.

Periods of intense activity were mixed with calmer days, generally in the first half of the week. If there was a lull, Robert announced, 'If anybody wants me I'll be at the bowling green'. But, like the others on the senior staff, he never stopped being a reporter. The gathering of news was his lifelong concern and he was active to the end; only two days before his death, at the age of ninety, he walked to Penrith cricket field to attend an opening ceremony.

CHAPTER 3

Going Courting

Courthouses varied little in internal appearance – the bench where proud JPs sat and listened, the dock, the witness box, the press seats and the well of the court where a big table was shared by the magistrates' clerk, his shorthand writer, the police prosecutor and solicitors for the defence. What gave the buildings their drawing power were the wide-ranging stories which unfolded of desperation and drama, stupidity and humour, greed and misfortune – a whole miscellany of the failings and weaknesses of the human race. Some of the frequenters of the courts – the testy JPs, policemen (some kindly but others officious), solicitors who might have made a fortune on the stage – added to the fascination.

Cases could be spiced with moments of inadvertent mirth. Within a couple of strokes of the reporter's pen, dull and repetitive evidence or legal submissions might suddenly give way to laughter in court.

A veteran village policeman had an entertaining style in the witness box. Giving evidence in a breach of the peace prosecution, he said: 'By the time I reached the scene outside the pub, a sizeable crowd had assembled, seconds had been appointed, the contestants had stripped for action and the main bout of the evening was about to begin.'

A young farm worker, who had been fined ten shillings for a minor motoring offence, stepped forward to pay the penalty – in the small chunky threepenny pieces in use in the 1950s. Indignantly the clerk to the magistrates swept the pile of coins aside and ordered the cheeky youth to go and get a more acceptable form of cash.

A farmer, on being found guilty of a tractor offence, disagreed fiercely with the verdict, initially refusing to pay, verbally abusing the JPs and finally flinging his cheque book at an official.

Magistrates in a distant part of the county, which I did not normally cover, were settling down to listen to a case of careless driving on the busy road which coursed past the front of the building. The faint throb of passing traffic provided the background as the defendant claimed from the witness box that the police had prosecuted the wrong man.

His words were suddenly interrupted by the chairman of the bench who snapped: 'Speak up, sir. We cannot hear a word.'

Surprised, the man raised his voice by several decibels: 'All of a sudden, I saw an approaching car which was cutting the corner . . .'

Yet again he was halted by the presiding magistrate who, rightly and fairly, pointed out that it was in the man's own interests to present his case in an audible way.

The din of raised voices finally prompted the magistrates' clerk to intervene. He held up a peremptory hand as a signal for the evidence to stop, and climbed up onto his own chair to bring himself level with the complaining magistrate, sitting on the raised bench. He immediately spotted the cause of the concern. 'Colonel,' he bellowed, leaning towards the elderly JP. 'Colonel, you are not plugged in.' A dislodged hearing aid was quickly put back into place and the court returned to normal. Over the years there were to be many more moments to cause smiles in the press seats.

Robert Irving and I walked through the busy streets of Penrith on market day. He was taking me to my first court, then held in part of the police station in Hunter Lane, a narrow, high-ceilinged building, with a wooden floor towards the front but with sandstone slabs making up the surface at the back. Policemen from the country stations sat there, waiting to give evidence, and workless men whiled away their time, listening to some of the spicier cases. In the press seats we joined Charlie Browning, the editor of the *Penrith Observer*, who wrote up the early cases, passing the copy to his junior, Dick Allen, who, at intervals, left the court to run the reports back to the printing works in Bishop Yards, to be set in type and included in a second edition of the Tuesday paper, which was printed around noon.

Only two cases really interested the reporters on that January morning in 1945. A farmer from the East Cumbrian Fellside was vehement in denying a charge of careless driving. His anger first showed as he took the oath. With every word, he

A glimpse of the spectacle of Appleby Assizes, last held in 1970. Uniformed trumpeters lead the way over the town bridge, heading for the court building at Shire Hall. The judge's Rolls Royce has a police escort.

slammed the Bible on the edge of the witness box – 'I (slam) swear (slam) by (slam) almighty (slam)' – until a court official managed to check him. The farmer's hurt innocence was of no avail and he handed over a pound note in payment of the fine in glowering silence.

A pub customer, a man in his twenties, blamed his lapse, in stealing the landlord's pocket watch from behind the bar counter, on the effects of his day-long drinking session. This sad case was to stick in my memory all my reporting life. Years afterwards, his son was to appear before the same court as a housebreaker and later still, at almost the last court I covered, a teenage youth faced a theft charge – he was the grandson of the befuddled drunk who lifted the publican's watch way back in 1945.

I was surprised by the range of misdeeds and sharp practices which put people before the courts. Even more surprising, though, was the realization that, as a reporter, I was sometimes more feared than the magistrates. Within the confines of a smallish town, where almost everybody knew everybody else, stains on the characters were in the newspaper reports and headlines and in some cases, the fines seemed almost secondary. I soon became accustomed to the out-of-court approach of men who had just been convicted of some form of dishonesty. One approach went something like this: 'If this business gets into the paper, it will kill my old mother. Personally, I couldn't give two hoots but please think of the effect on her.'

Distraught men seemed to forget their own folly and to blame the reporter: 'I'm finished if *you* put a report in the paper. I'll have to move somewhere else to have a hope of getting new work. It will split the family.'

This kind of pressure could never be acceded to, and became one of the most testing aspects of court work. Floods of tears made the pleas of women the most harrowing, for in some cases they were known to me. A moment of folly had ruined their lives. Or so it seemed to them in times of such utter depression.

Only occasionally did the non-publicity brigade turn to aggression. Outside the court at Hackthorpe, four young men pleaded with me to ignore the fact that they had just been convicted for siphoning petrol from parked cars. Two were known to me from my schooldays but I gave them the response that I would anybody else – that it was our duty to report, without exception. My return to Penrith along the A6 was eventful, and distinctly alarming, as the van containing the men repeatedly pulled across in front of my bicycle, in a clear attempt to knock me off, each of the swerves being accompanied by shouts of abuse. I was pleased to reach the safety of the office.

Just as some court 'customers' were in fear of publicity, there were a few who obviously relished the local notoriety which it gave them. Malcolm, who made a succession of appearances, mainly for excessive drinking, was an outgoing twenty-year-old who enjoyed a chat with the reporters. He boastfully produced a fistful of summonses, flicking through them and commenting, 'That was the one for Shap last week. No, that's to Appleby in a fortnight's time. Ah, here's today's.'

Although pubs and beer gave him his main leisure interest, he later discovered sex and was duly prosecuted for ' having carnal knowledge of ——— ———, she being a female under the age of sixteen years'. Brash and boastful, Malcolm described the encounter in the fullest detail, even disclosing that his unopposed love-making was performed in tune to a background of music from a nearby chapel. Organ music, you might say.

Although sex-related cases were by no means rife, several were deeply worrying. A young man travelled the countryside by motorbike in search of women alone. The feature common to his attacks was that they went no further than removing underwear. Eventually, he encountered a girl who was stronger and more determined than the rest and she overpowered him. When detectives visited his home they found drawers packed with knickers of all colours and descriptions, stolen either from washlines or by force.

The seemingly insatiable desire of some men to display their bodies was illustrated by the story of a man's return from prison, after serving a sentence for indecent exposure. Within hours, he went for a walk and practically the first people he saw, inside half a mile or so, were two swimwear-clad girls, sunbathing in a garden. What ensued was predictable, the umpteenth display of a lifelong weakness. Screams and a call to the police led to a swift arrest as the man made his way home. The girls, both foreigners, were leaving town on the next morning, so an evening court was arranged and the exhibitionist was on his way back to prison – less than twelve hours after getting home.

Man's weakness for offbeat behaviour is wide-ranging. The most difficult to detect is the raising of false fire alarms which can sometimes grow to epidemic proportions. The excitement of making a 999 call, the wail of the fire buzzer and the clang of the bell as the fire engine charged through the streets combined to cause an outbreak of these wasteful call-outs in Penrith during the fifties.

After weeks, the case was eventually solved because Deputy Chief Constable Louis Baum, in charge of the town police at the time, took his small dog for an evening walk. As the distant fire buzzer sounded its warning he saw a teenage youth in a phone kiosk he was passing. Instinct linked buzzer with boy. 'Wait a minute, son,' said the deputy chief as the youth started to run away – and, sure enough, the fire engine came into sight a few seconds later. The alarmist duly admitted all the other offences and, despite the penalties which were imposed, he made many more false calls in the years ahead, some locally, some in faraway places.

Oddly, the last I remember of him was many years later when an old town centre property caught fire late one night. The alarm-raiser of earlier times was sleeping rough in an upstairs room but was helped to safety by the very service which he had been such a nuisance to!

The sight of a burly police constable brandishing a bunch of long strips of paper was a sure sign that a case of lewd and indecent language was about to be heard – or, more precisely, semi-heard so far as the reporters were concerned! It seemed to me on these occasions that we were seen as a class apart, innocent types who must be protected from rude words and expressions. Spoken evidence was limited to setting the scene – often the gathering of an unruly crowd outside a pub, late in the evening – because the lewd language could not be uttered in open court.

'I then heard the defendant say this,' the PC told the court. He produced several strips of paper, with a few words typed on each, and passed them along the line of magistrates, to the clerk and to the accused man. Frustratingly, there was none of this spiciness for the reporters who could only sit in wonderment and study the faces of the JPs as they read the offending words. Was there just the hint of a smile on a couple of faces? And a faint blush on the cheek of the matronly woman at the end? Most of the magistrates put the papers aside quite quickly, as though to indicate distaste. The crude profanities of men outside public houses, late at night, were numerous, for more strips of paper might follow, though never to soil the thoughts and minds of innocent journalists. The fine of ten shillings was accompanied by a stern dressing-down, but our chasteness remained unsullied to the last.

In the heyday of the village bobby – Bill Cook at Low Hesket, Joe Dixon at Plumpton, George Southwell at Pooley Bridge and Harry Ingles at Langwathby, to name a few – late-night watches were kept on remote roads for lightless cyclists. They were often youngsters on their way home from country dances and one of them, a farmer's son who had sung a song or two with a dance band, gave the bobby his occupation as 'crooner'. So it appeared on the court list a week or two later. The errant bikers were generally fined five shillings per missing light, front and back. One offender was more fortunate than all the rest; he happened to appear before Penrith magistrates on VE Day and, in the spirit of the occasion, they told him to go and celebrate – there was no penalty.

Other late-night observations centred on country inns where after-hours drinking was suspected. These covert operations smacked of espionage, as burly officers concealed themselves close to pub windows, or lay on flat roofs with skylights, hoping to pick up tell-tale sounds from within the bar, possibly the clink of glasses or the splash of pints being poured. Scraps of conversation also went into police notebooks – 'One for the road? . . . OK, mine's a whisky . . . Just a laal drop o'rum if I might . . . Give him a Guinness.'

The drinking session was suddenly interrupted as the officers broke cover and burst into the bar. Landlords often claimed that no offence was being committed because it was a private party to celebrate a birthday, wedding anniversary or a big win on the horses.

The serious offences of murder, manslaughter, arson, rape, burglary and major fraud, among others, had to be dealt with at higher courts, the Assizes or Quarter Sessions, but there was always a considerable foretaste in the form of committal proceedings, held before the local magistrates to decide if there was 'a case to answer' at a higher level. Because they related to serious crime, often involving violence or sex, committals yielded very readable copy, although I felt that they often lacked balance and fairness.

Prosecution evidence was dictated and typed out and the depositions were signed by the witnesses, but defence or mitigation were seldom heard at this stage, with the accused man merely indicating that he wanted to reserve his defence. A great many of those sent for trial were guilty and pleaded so, although there could be cases of stigma hanging over innocent men, as a result of the preponderance of prosecution evidence taken when the allegations were initially heard by the magistrates, before the full trial. The old-style system of sending accused people for trial was lop-sided and unduly time-consuming. Present-day committals are both quicker and fairer, as the evidence usually gets its first full airing at the time of the trial. Outside a rural court I spoke to a young farmer, a man I had come across at social events. Wearing his best suit, he was obviously about to appear before the court. He assured me, however, 'My case won't take long. Driving under the influence of drink – I'll have to plead guilty, I haven't a cat in hell's chance.'

I was astonished an hour or so later when he walked into the courtroom with a solicitor who announced that my farmer friend would be denying the charge and that, as was his right, he wanted to be tried before a jury at the Quarter Sessions. Clearly, a chance meeting with the solicitor had brought about the change of heart.

At the subsequent trial I quickly realized why the farmer originally intended to plead guilty because the evidence against him was overwhelming: A car meandering along the road . . . the driver slumped at the wheel . . . the scientific analysis of a sample of urine showing a high alcoholic content. How could the man be innocent?

Yet his barrister got to his feet at the end of the prosecution and submitted, with great certainty, that there was no case to answer, pointing out the omission of a vital legal link involving the urine sample. Was the bottle filled by the farmer in the police station the same one as was later analysed in a Home Office laboratory? There was no evidence to show the samples were one and the same, as the officer who had posted away the specimen was not called to the witness box. The specimen analysed could have come from anybody. All the earlier talk of wobbly driving and drunken conduct became invalid, claimed the QC.

Not only was the case dismissed, but the farmer was awarded £25 to help pay for his defence. Outside, I asked him if he recalled what he had told me a month or so earlier, before the magistrates' court. He just smiled.

Twice a year, in the spring and the autumn, the law took on an extra tinge of colour and glamour when Assize courts were held at Carlisle and Appleby. We attended the Carlisle sittings only when there were local cases for trial but always went to Appleby because it was a spectacular occasion, steeped in the history of 700 years, even when it was a 'white glove' Assize, the gift of gloves to the presiding judge indicating that there was no criminal business.

The austerity of the courtroom in the Shire Hall contrasted with the flamboyance of the judge's drive through the little town in a gleaming Rolls Royce, headed by fanfare-blowing trumpeters in gold braided black jackets and escorted by white-gloved policemen. Appleby folk turned out in numbers to enjoy the bi-annual shows of pomp and ceremony. The courtroom, too, was generally full – certainly on the first day as the Clerk of Assize rose to read out the Queen's Commission of 'Oyer and Terminer and General Gaol Delivery and Assize'.

The last Appleby Assize was held in October 1970 when Judge Brabin offered words of condolence: 'Appleby has not experienced the growth and influx of people that other places have. It has not, therefore, experienced the increase in crime. Although Appleby has lost its Assize, the town has kept so much that when the balance is struck it may be thought that, in view of what has been retained, the forfeiture paid is worthwhile.'

Proud Appleby gloried in being an Assize town and it is doubtful whether its inhabitants agreed with the scarlet-robed judge!

If asked to recall the most memorable case I ever covered, I would have to include, high on the list, the famous defence of a jar of rum butter, Cumbria's best-known sweetmeat, heard in the Penrith courtroom in Hunter Lane. Representing a cafe proprietor, alleged to have sold rum butter which was deficient in its most vital ingredient, solicitor Brian Grainger armed himself with books of local recipes in preference to legal volumes.

The lawyer knew his way to a magistrate's heart. What clinched a successful defence was not eloquent oratory, but cartons of rum butter which were passed up to the JPs and enjoyed with evident relish.

There have been several cuts to the grassroots of justice over the past half-century. Of the six courts which I helped to report on as a junior, only Appleby and Penrith survive. The first to close was the distinctively spacious courthouse at Hackthorpe, with its two large fireplaces and a duty policeman at the door to bellow names across the A6 at the start of each new case. The former court building has become the 'Court Bar' for the pub next door.

Since the demise of Hackthorpe, the courts at Kirkby Stephen, Shap and Alston have also passed into oblivion, the result of a dubious trend towards the centralization of justice, defended as a saver of time and cash in belt-tightening days. The little courts epitomized everything that was right with the British judicial system because the JPs generally had a more intimate knowledge of the defendants, their characters and their circumstances. If they did err on a fine point of law, it was usually more than offset by sound Cumbrian common sense.

Film-makers created an image of these little courts as having been occupied by PC Plods and retired colonels with ear trumpets. The reality was much different, for out-of-town solicitors found that they could not pull the wool over the eyes of down-to-earth local magistrates, although the serious work of dispensing justice was occasionally enlivened by laughter in court.

When the Hackthorpe court was closed it was arranged that a picture should be taken of the JPs, the clerk, shorthand writer and policemen *in situ*, to accompany the *Herald*'s story. Engaged to take this historic picture was Penrith photographer Eric Davidson, a man of many talents and admirable qualities, although even he would agree that prompt timekeeping was not among them. When he did not present himself in court when the official business concluded, nobody was entirely surprised. However, the humour quickly wore thin as the magistrates, officials and others waited and waited. . . .

There was talk of 'issuing a warrant' to speed up the missing cameraman and, when he finally rushed into court, he was told that, in view of his late arrival, he must occupy the 'dock' while taking his picture. Entering into the spirit of the situation, Eric became the court's last 'defendant' and still took an excellent picture.

CHAPTER 4

Coffee Bar Contacts

Reporters are the eyes and ears of any newspaper. I admired the newsgathering abilities of my senior colleagues who, it seemed, simply strolled up King Street into the market square, chatted with friends and acquaintances for half an hour or so and returned to the office with the germ of a story. Robert Burne jotted down the brief details in his small, distinctive shorthand, often on the innards of a cigarette packet. This was later passed on to a younger reporter with orders to follow up the lead and the names of likely informants.

In the big city, people are strangers to each other, even if they live in the same street. In the small town or village, everybody knows everybody else – and therein lies the unique strength of the local weekly paper. Parish pump news, of which some speak in a despising way, is the lifeblood of papers like the *Herald*.

Reporters are not mere recorders of courts, council debates and annual meetings. They must be aware of ordinary folk, their problems and concerns, their successes and achievements.

No news spreads more swiftly than that of the dead and dying. The passing of a senior councillor, a bank manager, postmaster or prominent police officer would not be reported in a newspaper if they lived in Liverpool or London, but in Penrith, Keswick or Appleby there would be an eager inquiry from the local paper, for such men would merit at least half a column, plus a head-and-shoulders picture.

It is in the sphere of writing obituaries that the long experience of local reporters is priceless. If their service covers two or more generations, they can recall earlier days and achievements – of men who gained wartime gallantry awards, played in old-time dance bands, scored centuries as schoolboy cricketers or worked their way upwards in shops from errand boy to manager. I was made aware of this quality when Robert Irving, in writing about a veteran sportsman who had just died, gave colour and humour to the account by recalling that the man once played football with an elephant, as part of a publicity stunt for a circus which visited the town. The huge animal took up most of the goalmouth space but the Penrith hero still managed to score a goal with one of his three shots. When the 'contestants' reversed positions, the footballing elephant could not put the ball past his opponent who got a five pound note and a silver cup.

Invariably, the obituary was followed by a short report of the funeral. Within small communities there was great curiosity about the principal mourners and the senders of wreaths (generally described by the paper as 'beautiful floral tributes').

It was advantageous to mention the name of the undertaker, as such men were invaluable in tipping off the paper about deaths of noteworthy people.

The war was in its closing months when I began work but local servicemen were still being killed and injured. I was sent to gather paragraphs and, if possible, pictures of the casualties from their parents. My early fears about going into homes full of sorrow were totally needless. Many of the tears were tears of pride, and parents welcomed the chance of some form of public recognition of their sons. The experience prepared me for a career in which a lot of time was to be spent in researching and writing about the dead. Few families turned me away and most saw the reporter's visit as a mark of the worth of a loved one and they co-operated fervently.

'What about the accident on the A6 at Hackthorpe? Do you know who was killed?'

The question came from a woman counter assistant at Dayson's milkbar, a Penrith coffee shop which I visited as part of my newsgathering activities. In fact, this was my first knowledge of the crash but I quickly got hold of the news of a double fatality which the paper might otherwise have missed. In those far-off days the police did not put out official press statements about tragedies until all the details were known and late-week happenings could elude the papers unless they reached them via a grapevine of contacts. Dayson's, with a constant flow of customers and a talkative staff from all parts of town, was a hive of information and always worthy of a visit because of the stories which surfaced there. My twice-a-day calls were certainly rewarding – as well as building up an addiction for strong coffee (then only fourpence a cup, by the way!)

A sea of mud, over a foot deep in places, halted traffic on the A6 just north of Penrith in 1959. A thunderstorm of extraordinary ferocity hit the area, flooding houses, breaching walls and sweeping the top soil off cultivated land, carrying growing crops with it.

Some of the calls could be weirdly bizarre. I chatted over coffee with a long-known acquaintance, noticing as we did so the distinctive pattern on his green gumboots. A few hours later I was sent to the scene of a serious road accident just outside town. 'We don't know who he is yet,' said a young PC, indicating a body lying nearby, partly covered by a blanket. I experienced a unique eeriness when, on looking at the Wellington boots which protruded from beneath the cover, I suddenly realized that the crash victim was the jovial, vibrant man I had joked with only a few hours earlier.

My luckiest coffee bar encounter came some years after the closure of Dayson's, upon which The Tudor, along the street from the newspaper office, got quite a lot of custom. After a frustrating afternoon, trying to discover the identity of a major pools winner, I sought consolation in a cup of coffee.

The Tudor's only other customer at the time, the wife of a police contact, told me that her son had got home from school with the news that a classmate had confided in him that his father had just won a lot of money. We had our man!

A colleague, Bill Mossop, approached the lucky winner who agreed to drop the veil of anonymity and gave us the story.

What have we here? This is the sequel to a bizarre accident in which a pink bathtub on wheels collided with two cars at Kemplay Bank on the A6 just outside Penrith. The bath was named Sambo (Simply another motorised bath operation) and was en route from John O'Groats to Land's End with six young students in charge, as part of a charity bid. Constable Geoffrey Harrington put the 'vehicle' through a rigorous test before allowing it to continue towards Shap Fell.

Everybody a journalist knows is a potential contact or provider of stories, although not all of them appreciate the news value of what they see and hear. A minor accident on the A6, in which nobody was hurt, would be disregarded by most passers-by, but a former footballing associate called me when he saw that one of the vehicles involved was a motorized bathtub, in which a group of students were attempting a record-breaking journey. They welcomed the publicity and a photographer friend, Bob Armstrong, had great fun taking pictures of a motor patrol policeman road-testing the bath on wheels before allowing the students to resume their travels.

Weeks might pass without the hint of a major story to get the adrenaline throbbing again – then came drama at the double. A friendly fireman gave me an early morning tip-off that a house fire would have claimed the lives of two women but for the courage of a neighbour; he was a prominent local sportsman which made the story even better. Photographer Bob Armstrong took his pictures and I got an interview, packed with colourful quotes, and envisaged my story making the front page. As we left the hero's home, a local police inspector called us over. 'What are you doing here?' he inquired unexpectedly. 'You want to get out to Edenhall – there's been a murder there.'

Floods hit the delightful town of Appleby with spectacular ferocity. Melting

Penrith archer David Farrer was called in to help restore the telephone service between Penrith and neighbouring communities, severed when a 280-year-old stone bridge over the River Eden at Langwathby was swept away by severe floods during 1968. He used a bow and arrow to shoot a nylon cord over the river, some forty-five yards wide, to enable engineers to pull a line across and repair the connection.

snow on the fells at the head of the Eden Valley, coupled with prolonged pelting rain, turned the normally placid waters of the Eden into a raging torrent. As the river tore through the little town, it burst its banks and water surged into homes, pubs and shops. The scene was one of devastation, with the A66 through Appleby under feet of water and householders and shopkeepers striving to keep it at bay with brushes and sandbags. Personal stories abounded. Suitably clad, Bob Armstrong and I were in the thick of the action, picking up lively tales.

Then I called one of the national papers, to whom we were supplying some pictures and copy. The man on the newsdesk was quite blunt: 'You had better get to a place called Langwathby. That's where the real story is.'

Sweeping on down the valley, the floods had caused even more destruction, including the demolition of the stone bridge which carried the main Penrith-to-Alston road over the Eden, leaving only jagged central pillars and cutting off the principal route into town for the folk of Langwathby and nearby communities. The picture opportunities were even greater than those at Appleby, especially later in the day. A local archer, David Farrer, was called to the scene with his longbow to fire an arrow over the swollen river – a unique means of restoring the telephone link.

Another early morning call-out was to Clifton, just south of Penrith, where a main-line express had made an emergency stop and the passengers had been evacuated and taken to a village hotel. Cursing policemen made a thorough search of the train but, as in many such cases, the warning of a bomb aboard was mere mischief-making – a stupid prank which put passengers in terror and cost the ratepayers an immeasurable amount of money to pay for the turning out of fire engines and drafting in of policemen.

There was a quiver of thrilled uncertainty every time the phone bell rang, whether it was in the office or at dead of night. News does not always occur conveniently, between nine and five.

Life was enlivened by the thrill of the chase in following up leads, either by telephone or by going out to the scene, generally with Bob Armstrong, who was one of the most insatiable newsmen in the business. He went on to join BBC Television, working in the Newcastle studios, a career which was sadly to be cut short by his premature death.

Perhaps I should underline the fact that front page stories are only the spice on the cake of the weekly paper. Vital to the mix are the less tasty ingredients, the reports of countless small events and occasions. For the newspaper to play its full role in providing a complete news service, there are many happenings of a routine nature to be attended and covered – dinners, receptions, school speech days, presentations, public inquiries and, in particular, in the case of the *Herald*, annual meetings.

These yearly reviews were musts in my reporting days. They were spaced out throughout the calendar to tell the community at large of the ambitions, the achievements and the concerns of traders' associations, sports clubs, farmers' groups, gardening societies, local history bodies and the many other voluntary organizations which helped to make up the life of the town. The newspaper's aim was to give the facts, fairly and adequately, although we would always highlight any controversies – such as the spirited and suggestive debate by delegates at the county conference of Women's Institutes protesting about the lack of width and

Dinner at the George in the 1950s. Many town organizations chose the George Hotel, in the centre of Penrith, for their annual dinner or dinner-dance, and many still do.

length of bedsheets and urging manufacturers to make more provision for the tuck-in, in the interests of marital bliss. 'Many a divorce has been caused by too short a sheet', one woman pleaded.

Annual dinners were part of the winter calendar of events to be covered. In the immediate post-war years, with food still limited by rationing, they held a tolerable appeal for reporters with healthy appetites, although this tended to diminish in time. Each dinner occupied a full evening and, while the company was generally very sociable, the journalists could not enter into the full spirit of celebration, knowing that, while the rest of the diners were sleeping off any excesses, they faced the task of writing up the speeches.

The chamber of trade dinner, with customary toasts to 'The town and trade' and 'Our farmer friends', provided an annual guide to the local economy and was covered in some depth, as major stories were sometimes revealed. One after-dinner speaker, a county planner, blithely predicted a prosperous future for Penrith, with the population soaring to 30,000, but many years later the boom is still awaited. Other speeches were less compelling; one man droned on interminably until the toastmaster passed him a note advising: 'Shut up and sit down.'

Old boys' societies, sporting clubs and leagues, farmers' organizations and the British Legion all put on slap-up meals and good entertainment, although the artistes, as they were known, faced a tricky task in hitting just the right note with their suggestive stories. There could be shocked mutterings such as, 'The comedian went a bit far – though I liked the one about . . .'. Organizers were on safer ground with the stirring songs of Arnold Grieves and Ronnie Emmerson or Dr Jim Thomson with his tried and tested Cumbrian tales!

I viewed the annual banquet to the Mayor of Appleby with a certain degree of trepidation, as all the guests drank from a loving cup which, according to ancient tradition, was passed from mouth to mouth – a custom which began long before present-day anxieties about personal health and hygiene. A less formal get-together was the local firemen's annual supper but on at least one occasion the affair was thrown into disarray when they were called out to quell a blaze.

My fellow reporters were mainly local people, especially in the period from 1945 to 1965. In later years the tendency was to advertise any vacancies in the trade press and one or two national papers, although it is obviously helpful if newcomers have a knowledge of the area.

George Hobley and Frank Shaw, who were reporters prior to the war, returned to the staff after service in HM Forces and advanced through the ranks to become editors of distinction. As the years passed, new reporters generally came directly from Penrith Grammar School, like brothers Kenneth and Norman Nicholson, Frazer Lindsay and Bill Mossop, plus Ross Brewster, from Keswick, and Roger Davis, the only newcomer from outside the county. All these men eventually moved to other papers, apart from Bill Mossop who, years later, became managing director.

For many years the woman reporter was as rare as the woman doctor or the female councillor. Nowadays she is accepted as an integral part of every newspaper. Editors appreciate that a big part of the readership is feminine and the woman of the 1990s is interested in all the columns of the papers, even in sport.

Eyebrows were raised in the *Herald* reporters' room on 5th April 1956 when Evelyn Rae became the first lady journalist – a woman in what had been an all-male domain for nearly a century.

When she was engaged as a £4-a-week junior reporter, Evelyn was lectured by editor George Hobley and manager Robert E. Burne on the importance of upholding the good name of the *Herald* — a fine newspaper and a household name. She was expected to be well-behaved and moral at all times.

Four years earlier she had saved another girl from drowning in the River Eden. The resultant news item in the *Herald* made her think of journalism as a career. She was an effervescent girl of great motivation, who quickly earned the respect of colleagues and made a distinctive contribution, as well as giving the place a bit of glamour.

Her twelve years as a reporter left Evelyn with many memories: travelling to jobs with photographer Eric Davidson who in freezing weather carried a paraffin lamp in his car to provide a degree of warmth . . . being invited to look at the corpse when gathering details for an obituary . . . visiting 10 Downing Street for an exclusive interview with the wife of Prime Minister Harold Wilson (Mary Wilson formerly lived at Penrith while her father was a Congregational Church minister in town).

CHAPTER 5

Ullswater Hero

The new *Bluebird* arrived at Ullswater in January 1955, although I had already admired the sleek lines of the powerful speedboat when she was unveiled to over a hundred newspapermen in a factory at Samlesbury, Blackburn, the previous November.

An attempt to break the world water speed record was something new for Ullswater. Most of the previous bids in this country had been made on Coniston Water, in southern Lakeland, first by the late Sir Malcolm Campbell and then by his son, Donald, both in an earlier, less forceful *Bluebird*.

With the emergence of the second version, a £25,000 turbo-jet hydroplane, attention switched to Ullswater where Donald Campbell's next record attempt was to be made. He had the encouragement of the MP and businessman Sir Wavell Wakefield, who had just purchased the shares of a Penrith chemist named Charlie Dixon to gain control of the Ullswater Navigation and Transit Company which operated two lake pleasure boats, *The Lady of the Lake* and the *Raven*.

The prospect of big crowds thronging the lakeshore was viewed with some alarm by local people who enjoyed the peacefulness of an Ullswater sunset, but many others thrilled with eager anticipation at the prospect of seeing the daring and determined Campbell in action.

Bluebird was transported under police escort to a new boathouse at Glenridding, at the head of the lake. That was when I first met Leo Villa, the chief mechanic, who was in charge of the preparation of the speedboat in readiness for Campbell's arrival. The fifty-five-year-old Cockney had an excellent rapport with the press and, despite the demands of his exacting job, he could generally find time to help young reporters who had only slight knowledge of jet engines and the history of high-speed travel on water. His experience of the business stretched back to 1922 and he had figured in record attempts with both Campbells, father and son. 'Imagine motoring over ice at high speed', he said.

There was an early problem when it was found that a wooden slipway, constructed by local joiner Tom Craig, could not be placed flat on the lakebed because of a sandbank a few yards from shore. Patterdale's fire brigade came to the rescue, using a high powered jet to shift the obstruction.

The neighbouring villages of Glenridding and Patterdale, at the head of the lake, revelled in the fleeting fame. Residents showed their support for Donald Campbell by throwing a party in his honour in the village hall, with speeches of welcome and gifts of lucky tokens to the young hero and his team. There was

Bluebird at speed on Ullswater during the days leading up to the attempt on the water-speed record.

immense pride in the fact that the speed bid was being made on *their* lake by a man they quickly got to know and like.

The attempt began in earnest on 10th February, 1955. Campbell's twenty-six-year-old wife, Dorothy, smashed a quart bottle of champagne on the prow of the boat and said: 'I name this boat *Bluebird*. May God bless her, her pilot and all who work on her.'

With Donald in the cockpit, the craft was towed out onto Ullswater for the first slow-speed trial run. As she moved away from the boathouse and, eventually, out of sight, astute newspapermen positioned themselves near a radio monitor station on the shoreline, in the hope of picking up snatches of the conversation passing between the pilot and his mechanics, who were in accompanying launches.

'OK, boys. Here we go,' shouted Donald Campbell, but his initial jubilation soon gave way to anxiety. The lake was like 'a choppy sea' in parts, water was entering the air intakes and the fear was that this would damage the turbine.

Waiting newsmen passed word of the problems to their papers while the tests were still in progress. They were in something of a dilemma when Campbell got back to the boathouse and described the trial as 'quite satisfactory under the conditions'. Some stories were amended but, even so, the talk of possible damage, reported in a few papers on the next day, cast something of a shadow on the Glenridding scene.

Many modifications had to be made to *Bluebird* in the first couple of months and it was soon clear that an early result was out of the question. It was mid-March before Donald Campbell could make his first trial runs at speed, topping 100 mph. On the strength of this, an estimated 6,000 spectators turned up the following weekend. They were disappointed when a high wind, coupled with more alterations, ruled out another immediate show of great speed.

There was much better news in April when the young speed ace was interviewed on the BBC's *Sports View* by Brian Johnston and spoke of the value of wind tunnel tests being carried out with a model of his boat. With these completed, he would soon be ready for further runs on the lake.

It was during July that the record attempt neared its climax and public interest intensified dramatically. Never before had there been such a spate of traffic on the roads on both sides of Ullswater. On the long evenings every nook and cranny was occupied by the cars of people hoping to catch sight of the speeding boat. George Hobley captured the atmosphere in an editorial in the *Herald*:

> It was as if the world and his wife, and the family as well, were determined to make the most of the occasion, even it if meant a long wait in the sun in the hope of catching a glimpse of the speedboat.

Press cameras click as Mrs Dorothy Campbell christens the speedboat Bluebird *at Glenridding, Ullswater – a prelude to Donald Campbell's successful attempt to break the World water-speed record in 1955.*

As the day drew on, the more restless might tend to feel a little frustrated when *Bluebird* failed to show her paces but, after all, the evening air was balmy, there were lovely views to look at and plenty of people to talk to – and there was always tomorrow.

On the improvised parking ground at Glenridding the cars were lined up, row upon row. The village street and the road to the landing stage were thronged with people from morning to night, and cafes and shops did a roaring trade.

Among the vast crowds of onlookers, the reporters and photographers, newsreel and television cameramen could be spotted because of their apparent disinterest. They were a race apart from the masses of holidaymakers – small groups of them, talking and smoking endlessly as the time dragged on from morning to evening . . . waiting, waiting, waiting. Their apparent detachment was simply the patience of men who had been through it all before in widely varying locations and circumstances – hanging about waiting for something to happen and then working at high pressure when it did.

A cheerful Donald Campbell at the controls of his record-breaking Bluebird.

Donald Campbell (centre) discusses arrangements for his 1955 record attempt with Sir Wavell Wakefield, chairman of the Ullswater Navigation and Transit Company, and a supporter of the bid. On the left is local joiner Tom Craig, who made the slipway for Bluebird.

When the big day, 23 July 1955, finally arrived I missed out. It was a Saturday, always a busy day for weekly papers, and I was covering either Shap rose fête or Appleby British Legion sports as Donald Campbell raced into the record books. The plum job of reporting the triumphant attempt went to my colleague, Frank Shaw who had shared the earlier coverage with George Hobley and myself. His story was headlined over five columns: World water speed record broken on Ullswater . . . Mr. Donald Campbell averages 202.32 mph . . . 'Just another trial run' turned out to be fastest ever.

'The roar of the jet wound up to a high-pitched howl,' wrote Frank Shaw. *Bluebird* shot down the course with a long finger of spray like a furry tail.'

Hopes soared when it became known that the speed over the first run was 215.08 mph. Although the return journey was rather slower, the speed of 189.57 mph was enough to break the record of 178.49 mph set some years before by the American Stanley Sayers in *Slo Mo Shun*.

Bluebird, *with Donald Campbell in the cockpit, being towed on to Ullswater for the first trial runs in 1955.*

Bluebird *at speed on Ullswater.*

'I am glad to have been able to follow the old skipper and bring this record back to England,' said Donald Campbell. His wife, Dorothy, and his mother, Lady Campbell, embraced him. Leo Villa and the rest of the mechanics joined in the jubilation.

The excitement, which had mounted over six months, quickly died. Gone were the big crowds and traffic-packed roads. *Bluebird* was repainted before being moved from Glenridding to Blackpool, to be shown off to thousands of holidaymakers by the seaside.

Donald Campbell left the furnished house which he had taken in Glenridding but he was long remembered by the dalesfolk, not so much as a breaker of records, but as a modest and pleasant fellow who attended functions, chose beauty queens, presented cups and left behind the Campbell Trophy, to be awarded annually to the best local sportsman of the year.

Over the next nine years Donald Campbell and *Bluebird* pushed up the record six times – at Lake Mead, Nevada; four times on Coniston Water; and finally at Perth, Western Australia, where he registered 276.33 mph.

It was this record which he set out to break on 4th January 1967, back at Coniston, when his jet-powered boat crashed and sank – a sad, sensational and spectacular end to a career of courage and commitment.

CHAPTER 6

Sporting Pride

'Come on you bonny Blues,' they yelled from the soccer sidelines. 'Well played, Penrith.'

My vivid memory of reporting sport as a teenager is of the local patriotism which the matches engendered – a heart-warming glow of pride, a feeling of togetherness, an all-embracing belief in the community we lived in. Elderly and middle-aged men, impressionable youngsters and a surprising number of women cheered on Penrith's football teams, not necessarily because they were soccer fans, but because they were Penrithians and fiercely loyal to their town.

The same feeling of 'Our town forever, right or wrong' applied throughout the circulation area . Whatever the sport, people would support *their* team unfailingly. They belonged to a generation brought up long before the arrival of television and their heroes were not the much publicized and richly rewarded men of national sport but the likes of Charlie Short, the powerful centre forward who scored 102 goals in a single season, and the dashing young cricketer Harold Millican, who captained the county team as well as the town side and smote the ball as though intent on knocking the cover off. 'If you are going to flash, flash hard' was a saying which summed up his forthright approach to the summer game.

Those were golden days for sport at local level. The following of football was so fanatical that when an overnight snowstorm threatened a major cup-tie at Penrith, scores of men turned up with spades and brushes and cleared the pitch so that the match could go ahead.

The great team of the immediate post-war years – Byers; Seery, Bell, J.; Bell, A., Branthwaite, Richardson; Stout, Boustead, Short, Donaldson, Docker – figured in a remarkable succession of hard-fought draws with the men of West Auckland, in County Durham, to settle which club should advance to the next round of the FA Amateur Cup. Incredibly, the teams battled it out five times, the matches lasted 8½ hours overall and the goals scored totted up to 23 by the time Penrith finally triumphed.

The scorelines of the cup-tie marathon were phoned through to the *Herald* to be displayed in the front office window. Enthusiasm was such that, as half-time or full-time approached on some distant football field, crowds built up in King Street, with townsfolk slipping away from office desks and shop counters to get the latest news. As that outstanding season progressed, our heroes won the championship of a Carlisle-based league and lifted the county cup for the first time ever. The successes inspired a bold decision by the club to seek membership of the much stronger Northern League, centred on the North-East. The crowds of over 2,000, who watched the matches, were remarkable, seeing that the town's population was only around 10,000.

I was caught up by the wave of enthusiasm as I covered the matches. My regret was that, with newsprint still rationed and papers limited in size, the reports were often printed in six point, the smallest typeface, for several years. This did not seem to do justice to the team's triumphs or the zest of the supporters.

An early report led to a stern reprimand because I suggested that the referee should have worn the colours of the opposition, so biased were many of his decisions. The fans clearly shared my view but a strong protest from the official, with talk of solicitors' letters, made me more guarded in my comments after that.

My teachers at Penrith Grammar School had taught me clean-cut English but, as a young reporter, I felt under a handicap because I knew little of the traditional clichés of the coverage of the game – well-worn words and expressions such as 'leathern spheroid' (ball), 'custodian' (goalkeeper), 'leader ploughed a lone furrow' (centre forward had no support), 'attack lacked method and cohesion'

Rugby Union has been played in Penrith since the last century, although the present club was formed in 1921. Penrith (in the striped jerseys) were playing Old Creightonians (Carlisle) when this picture was taken on the Foundry field in the 1950s. The club now plays matches at Winters Park, on the outskirts of town.

(played aimlessly), 'showed a clean pair of heels but was wide of the target' (did everything but score), 'defensive tactics were not appreciated by spectators' (crowd booed a dirty fullback) and 'cleared his lines under pressure' (belted the ball out of the ground). I quickly learned some of these ancient sayings – and still regret the fact!

Initially bereft of stereotyped terms, I was tempted to turn to the sports columns of the daily newspapers for inspiration. One of the top reporters, in describing a famous player of the day, used the phrase, 'His football brain ticking over merrily'. At 16, this description so appealed to me that I inserted it in one of my match reports, applying it to Tommy Boustead, a Penrith inside forward of great skill and cunning. Sub-editor Irving did not speak to me of this obvious plagiarism but brought me back to the reality of the *Herald* by striking out the words I had cribbed and substituting, 'Boustead played well'.

My working relationship with Robert Irving was strengthened by a shared interest in sport. He was almost fifty years older and a journalistic father-figure to me, but when the conversation turned to football or cricket, the age gap diminished immeasurably. He saw in me an assistant and, ultimately, a successor in writing of the sporting scene. He had a lifelong devotion to football, in particular, which stemmed from playing for a junior team many years before, although he always belittled his own skill. Robert's work for the game, mainly as an administrator, covered many years, at both town and county level, and late in his long life the Football Association gave him a special medal.

Penrith's advance to the Northern League enabled me to boost my income by means of freelance earnings. At Robert Irving's suggestion, I wrote to the sports editors of the North-East papers, several of whom took up my offer to cover Penrith's home matches for them.

While this gave me rather more cash, and more experience of working under pressure, the money was extremely hard earned. Of the three evening papers I was to serve, two – at Darlington and Middlesbrough – requested 200 or 150 words at quarter-time, a further 100 at half-time, generally 50 or 75 at threequarter-time and the result, with additional scorers, at the final whistle. The Sunderland paper was less demanding in terms of words but calls had to be made at half-time and full-time.

To say that this was a challenging task is a masterpiece of understatement because in those far-off days there wasn't a telephone on the soccer ground. Stamina was tested as I ran the 300 yards to a phone box in a nearby street, notebook in hand, hoping against hope that my series of transfer charge calls would not be delayed because the kiosk was already in use, possibly by a talkative housewife. Inevitably, these departures from the ground meant that I missed parts of the play and, although updates were given by friendly fans or by a local shopkeeper, Jack Varty, who compiled match reports for the rival *Penrith Observer*, the arrangement was far from ideal. Before long I was forced to get an assistant, paying one of my brothers, a friend or girlfriend to do the running and make the calls.

Vocal support of the town cricket was much more restrained, as befitted the sport of gentlemen, except for mid-week knock-out matches – limited-overs

Cricket at Penrith in the 1950s was given added spice by knock-out competitions and seven-a-side matches. These top-hatted and bewhiskered men were among the contestants, aided and abetted by a young woman. Front (left to right); Harold Edmondson, Jackie Lancaster, Miss Hill, Louis Rigby, Roly Kirkbride. Back; Wally Rylands, Jim Airey, Jonathan Stalker.

encounters between sides consisting partly of novices. There were many big hits and much adventurous running between the wickets, but the appeal lay, not in the cricket itself, but in the comical wisecracks shouted from 'The Wall'. It was traditional for many of the onlookers to lounge against the wall which divided the ground from the passing lane (now a road because of the town's expansion).

The cricket was lively and entertaining but the main source of fun was the barracking which may have upset more sensitive players but was revelled in by hundreds of spectators. The king of the barrackers was Jack Lancaster – 'Jackie Lank' to the fans – whose shouted comments gave a new dimension to cricket-watching.

'I hope "Lank" is in good form tonight,' said spectators, as though the vocal accompaniment was more of a treat than the competition itself. The barrage of quips was practically non-stop. The outfielder who put down a catch was a popular target. 'Git him a swill,' bellowed Jackie (a swill being Cumbrian for a large basket used in agriculture). If a batsman got himself run out through tardiness in covering the 22 yards between the stumps, the spectators chuckled as the star barracker informed him: 'Thoo's aboot as lish as a wood wagin' (lish being the dialect word for agile).

A police chief, whose middle stump was uprooted before he could score a run, tried to put on a brave face, smiling resolutely as he strode back towards the pavilion. Jackie was no respecter of high authority. 'Thoo can smile,' he shouted. 'Thoo can smile but thoos bleeding inwardly.'

Other collectors of 'ducks' were reminded that, when roasted, they tasted better with a spot of apple sauce. Embarrassing interruptions would have been frowned upon at Lord's or Old Trafford but at Penrith they were essential to the appeal on long evenings. We lounged in the sun, bought tuppenny ice creams from John Wood, from a nearby shop, and laughed at the unique commentary on the knock-out matches.

Offended cricketers suggested to 'Jackie Lank' that his efforts as a player would be no better than theirs. 'We'll see aboot that,' he responded. He got together his own team, the Barrackers, and, although they failed quite miserably at the first attempt, some judicious additions to the batting strength (including county skipper Harold Millican) enabled the irrepressible Jack to lead his team to victory after several years. This achieved, he retired from active involvement and went back to his customary perch behind the wall.

Although football attracted much greater support, cricket was richer in characters and quirky happenings. The town's watchmaker, Fred Barclay, a lifelong member of the Penrith club, regaled me with stories of more primitive

In the Eden Valley of Cumbria there are many delightful cricket fields such as the tree-surrounded ground at Appleby which nestles in a bend of the river. A net is part of the equipment; to retrieve the ball when big hitters send it flying into the water!

days and a host of colourful characters. There were occasional flare-ups to disturb the general gentility of the cricket scene in his days as a player: a heated altercation during a match in the grounds of Greystoke Castle so angered Lady Mabel Howard, the Lady of the Manor, that she chased the players from the grounds and told them never to return. With no flags or ropes to make the boundaries on village fields, Fred, as captain of the town's second team, strolled round with the home skipper to discuss whether a hit to or beyond a particular haycock merited two runs or three.

Penrith cricketers achieved a great deal of success in the fifties, winning a county league five times in eight seasons, but it was the offbeat and the unusual which made the biggest imprint on the sports reporter's memory. One village batsman seemed set to make a big score until he insisted upon retiring, explaining that he must get back to the farm, as it was his turn to milk the cows. Other enforced departures were by players and umpires who were also fire-fighters and dashed away when the warning buzzer wailed, whatever the state of play.

A Penrith player, George Veitch, once contrived to play in two matches at the same time, racing across the school campus which separated the cricket fields to bat and bowl in both of the games. When one of the national dailies got hold of the story the reporter was not content with the straight version but added ridiculous embellishments, one to the effect that the hero dashed back and forwards through crowded town centre streets, wearing a club blazer and tasselled cap. What was a cracking story in its own right was needlessly thrust into the world of make-believe.

The tang of freshly-cut grass, mixed with the smell of athletes' embrocation and a hint of tea brewing from a mobile canteen . . . the purring precision of a military band . . . the white coated bellman with bell at the ready . . . runners jogging laconically round the track . . . the backcloth of the rugged slopes of Butter Crag, soon to test the stamina and the courage of the fell runners . . . . Grasmere sports dawned again.

Summer sport reached a high point of physical endeavour, endurance and excellence with the great outdoor athletic meetings each July and August – at Ambleside, Keswick, Penrith, Pooley Bridge and 'Glorious Grasmere', matchless in setting and tradition. The Lake District specialities – fell races, hound trails and wrestling in the distinctive Cumberland and Westmorland style – gave these events a Cumbrian uniqueness and made sporting heroes of farmers, shepherds and other men of the dales.

Grasmere's historians, Hugh Machell and Canon Hardwicke Rawnsley, summed up the aims of the great gathering as being 'to improve the nobility of physique, in praise of bon camaraderie and friendly emulation, to promote honest rivalry in athletics, to inspire enthusiasm amongst lovers of wrestling, to increase the speed and sturdiness of hounds, to encourage climbers of our rugged fells, to give a stimulus of the nimbleness of agile pole leapers and high leapers.'

I was lucky to report Grasmere in the heyday of some of the greats of Lakeland sports. My unfading memory is of Bill Teasdale, the Caldbeck shepherd and fell running champion of the fifties, as he bounded down Butter Crag, pulling away from the rest of the racers and then pelting into the arena, with head thrust

Glorious Grasmere. An air of expectancy pervades the famous sports arena, in the heart of the Lake District, as the leader in the fell race, a lone figure in white, bounds down the lower slope, less than a minute from victory. Hound trails and wrestling in the Cumberland and Westmorland style are other traditional features of Grasmere sports.

Who's first? Judges of the 100 yard sprint at Grasmere sports in August 1967 deliberated for ten minutes before deciding on the placings. Jackie Cunningham, Workington (second from left), was adjudged to have taken the tape from Ivor McAnany, Blyth, on the left, and Frank Foster, Benwell, on the extreme right.

forward and arms pumping, as the crowd rose and the band struck up with 'John Peel'. He always seemed the freshest man to finish and, while following competitors crashed to the turf in sheer exhaustion, Teasdale calmly collected his dentures from a trainer to be ready to face the press photographers.

They called Bill the 'King of the Fells' but he was an unassuming monarch and attributed his success to the fact that he climbed the hills above Caldbeck every day in life while watching the sheep flocks. His remarkably slow heart beat was believed to be another factor.

Old-timers used to say: 'There'll nivver be another wrustler leike Geordie Steadman'. He was a Grasmere immortal of the nineteenth century, a winner of countless titles, cups and belts, and a heavyweight of massive proportions with a chest measurement of 51½ inches and a thigh of 25½ inches. However, with the passage of time there were other giants, not only in physique but in reputation, who dominated Grasmere, as the 'mother ring' of wrestling in the distinctive Cumberland and Westmorland style. Men like George Lowden, Tom Kennedy, Tom, Joseph and Ralph Pooley, Douglas Clark and, in the post-war era, Ted Dunglinson loomed large literally, as well as metaphorically, in the wrestling rings. They drew vast crowds in the pre-eminent age of the sport – an age which faded with the arrival of counter attractions like the car and, in particular, the television. Sadly, this enabled national and international athletes to overshadow our home-grown heroes.

A reminder from 1961 of Penrith Gala, held in an idyllic setting just outside Pooley Bridge, Ullswater. The sports meeting, which became defunct many years ago, comprised foot and cycle races, wrestling in the local style, hound trails and fell races. The wooded hill in the background is Dunmallard.

In my personal 'hall of fame' of Lakeland athleticism there must also be a place for Joseph Watson – 'Joss' to the crowds – a builder from the village of Newbiggin (Stainton), near Penrith, who became an institution of post-war Grasmere, specializing in jumping events, but taking time out to compete in sprints, from the 1947 revival right through to the mid-nineties. It says much for his personal resilience that at the height of his career as a high jumper and pole vaulter 'Joss' crashed down onto sun-baked turf, rather than the well-cushioned landings enjoyed by today's top athletes. He may not have achieved outstanding success in more recent times but deserves a special niche if only for competing when aged over seventy.

It is not being unkind to say that the wrestling fraternity tend to see themselves as a breed apart at Grasmere. Fell runners and sprinters may have the rest of the crowd in a frenzy of excitement but the eyes of the wrestling men seldom stray from the bouts in progress. An elderly wrestling official was so engrossed in his

Ready for the off . . . . Starter Wilf Tallentire raises his blunderbuss to send runners on their way in the fell race at the village sports at Croglin. Nearest to the camera is 'King of the fells' Bill Teasdale, the shepherd from Caldbeck, who won many Cumbrian fell races in the 1940s and 1950s.

sport, and unaware of what was taking place in the arena at large, that he wandered across the track, causing a serious pile-up of speeding cyclists, but somehow escaping personal injury. I was fascinated by the language of the wrestlers, such as 'takking hod' (the getting to grips of rival contestants) and the various 'chips' used in felling opponents — the backheel, the hank, the twist off the breast, twist off the hip and the full buttock.

Grasmere in the sunshine was probably the peak of my journalistic year in terms of personal enjoyment - but, oh when it rained! A cloudburst over the sports ground in the fifties sent competitors and spectators scurrying for shelter. Lying nearby to me was a canvas bag, normally used to protect the announcer's microphone, and, in my anguished desperation, I grabbed this cover from the ground and pulled it over my head, for protection from the downpour, not realizing that it was almost full of rainwater. I was both drenched and embarrassed, as colleagues and my wife-to-be had seen the episode from the shelter of the press box. I was never allowed to forget.

The sports at Keswick – sadly now defunct – drew the August Bank Holiday Monday crowds. Appearance money was paid to attract top overseas athletes, such as Barney Ewell from the USA and Eric Cummings from Australia, but

Hounds away! Dogs stream away at the start of a hound trail, one of the traditional sports of the Lake District. The setting was near Mungrisdale, between Penrith and Keswick, where the village sports were in progress. Heavy betting takes place on the results of the aniseed-scented trails.

there were also home-grown runners of note. I can still picture John Brough, a quarter-miler of silky style, moving round the track with grace and power, like a finely-tuned machine leaving so many steamrollers and toiling trucks in his wake. He was the most elegant runner I have ever seen on a Cumbrian track but somehow – possibly because he was local, from Penrith – he never quite received the accolades he merited. I christened him 'the purple flash' because of the coloured strip he favoured.

Farmers' meadows became sports arenas in many villages for one day a year, with cowpats removed and replaced with sawdust, circular tracks marked out with wooden pegs and flags, and tents erected for runners and cyclists to change in. Although the settings were unlikely, the going could be rough (especially for speeding bike riders) and the prize money was limited, these little gatherings provided rural fun and an opportunity for athletes to prepare for the bigger events. In the fifties the programmes sometimes included old penny pitching, bowling for a pig, quoits, tug-of-war and pillow fight, as well as the more commonplace footraces, cycle races and wrestling.

In some villages, sports day coincided with the final of a football knock-out competition, held over long summer evenings in the preceding weeks. Big crowds turned up for these brawn-versus-brain tussles, in which village lads used their superior strength and out-and-out, win-at-all-costs enthusiasm to counter the skills of more gifted performers, top local footballers who normally played in the county leagues. I figured in a drawn match between a side representing a Penrith pub and a team of lusty village lads. On the following morning three of the pub

Since this picture was taken, showing yachts and other craft on Ullswater, a speed ban has been introduced, putting an end to water skiing.

team were receiving treatment for injuries in the local cottage hospital. Our captain bluntly declined a replay, telling the organizers, 'If that's the way they play, they can have the b . . .'.

Some of the sports meetings were further enlivened by gymkhanas, horse and pony races and motorbike events. Even in the 1950s there were allegations that competing horses were being 'doped', by the injection of drugs, and the local governing body warned that saliva tests would be taken from the animals.

One of the most scurrilous bits of race-fixing I can recall was at a sports meeting at a remote village in the Eden Valley, and was aimed at extracting money from the bookmakers. Some fell runners conspired to make sure that the race was won by an outsider because betting odds on him were more rewarding. The race which followed was a ludicrous spectacle, with the chosen 'winner' so inadequate that the set-up became obvious. Some of the other competitors tripped over non-existent obstacles and faltered at walls which they would normally have scaled with ease; one much fancied runner disappeared from sight altogether until the unlikely victor finally stumbled over the finishing line.

The attitude was that such skullduggery was acceptable because the only sufferers were the bookies. They were tight-lipped as they paid out the ill-gotten gains.

Sport briefly threatened the peace and tranquillity of a beauty spot of the *Herald* circulation area. Increasing numbers of water-skiers turned Ullswater into a lake for physical enjoyment, rather than quiet contemplation. When the annual national championships of the sport took place there in 1961 the paper reported that the lakeside road was choked with cars and spectators. Editor George Hobley raised the first doubts about the lake's change of character and in the fullness of time a ban was imposed on the speeding motorboats which the skiers relied on. Countless Cumbrians love sport but the transformation of a lovely lake was too high a price to pay.

CHAPTER 7

What a Welcome for Wilfred

Cheering crowds, the town band playing with pride, a welcoming banner and civic dignitaries lined up on the station platform . . . .

Such an impressive turn-out must surely have been to honour the arrival of a royal personage, a foreign dignitary or a leading film star. But no – the small Eden Valley town of Appleby turned out in force to greet Wilfred Pickles, quiz-master, comedian and newsreader!

In the 1950s the glib Pickles was in radio entertainment as big a star and personality as many of the revered performers and interviewers who were to dominate television screens in later years. We were less blasé in those days and looked on the top broadcasters of the time with affection and adulation. They were heard but seldom seen, certainly not in the flesh.

The popularity of Wilfred Pickles sprang from the homely appeal of his weekly quiz show, *Have a Go*, half an hour of interviews with local characters, spiced with droll questions about embarrassing moments and advice on guarantees of wedded bliss. Stirring this rich mixture of good humour and titillating chatter were Pickles and his buxom wife, Mabel, whose familiar retort, 'You're a cheeky monkey', in reply to some intimate question, always brought the house down. Wilfred invariably posed the question: 'Are you courting?'

The hero worship the couple enjoyed was such that I spent most of a day covering the visit and the star treatment the couple received. Mayor Frank Betts and town clerk Tom Longstaff, with their wives, made up the welcoming group. The town band was also there and led Wilfred's taxi through crowded streets, accompanied by two men carrying a 'Welcome to Wilfred' banner.

The crowds continued to cheer outside the town's main hotel until Wilfred appeared at a window and waved to them. He really could have been a royal visitor, so generous was the greeting. Next day, the reporters and photographers followed Mr and Mrs Pickles on their image-making travels in and about the town, first to two schools and then to an old people's home to meet some of their greatest fans.

The visit was probably the first time I saw public relations in action. A spot of fishing in the Eden with ninety-three-year-old Tom Howe had little to do with catching a trout but everything to do with drawing in press

'Who's taking this picture, buddy?' Photographer Bob Armstrong found a rival in Bing Crosby, the American crooning star, who was on a visit to Greystoke Castle while enjoying a spot of fishing in Cumbria. In the centre of the group are his hosts at the castle, Stafford and Gracia Howard.

photographers, as Wilfred, in angler's garb, posed with the old man on the bank of the river.

When Appleby went 'on the air' for the first time, by means of the Pickles quiz show, 400 townsfolk crowded into the public hall, with an overspill of 200 in a school hall. Community spirit was aroused because this was a bit of local history – a first-ever opportunity to see the BBC in action – and, after all, for half an hour the nation's interest was to focus on their town, on the deeds, misdeeds and witticisms of their friends and neighbours.

Prepare to be impressed while I drop a few more big names from a past era. Any visit to the circulation area by a nationally known figure generally enlivened the front page in those far-off, more impressionable times. PC Matt Armstrong, the bobby at Pooley Bridge, at the northern tip of Ullswater, phoned in to say that a motorist who approached him to check the route to Penrith was actor Sir Laurence Olivier, accompanied by his wife, Vivien Leigh. Their presence was duly recorded under the headline of 'Stage stars at Ullswater'.

My first encounter with stardom was on the platform at Penrith railway station where I talked to ten-year-old John Howard Davies – 'a fragile, angelic-looking child with shining fair locks' – who was on a personal appearance tour to publicize *Oliver Twist*, the film in which he took the title role, late in the 1940s. Then there were the American crooner Johnny Ray, surrounded by fans; the eighteen-year-old King Hussein of Jordan, who fell ill during a holiday stay at Keswick; film stars

Coco, the famous clown, chatted with reporters during a visit to Penrith to open an event for the Evergreen Club in the 1950s. The journalists were Joe Gregory, Penrith Observer, *and, on the right, John Hurst,* Herald.

Trevor Howard and Jean Simmons shooting scenes for *The Clouded Yellow* on Ullswaterside; comedian Frankie Howerd, wearing dark glasses in a bid to remain incognito at an agricultural show; an early star of the *Coronation Street* soap opera; ukulele-playing comedian George Formby, who came to buy pedigree Shorthorn cattle; Coco the clown, complete with circus greasepaint, when opening an old folks' money-making event; curly-haired Charlie Drake, of 'Hello my darlings' fame, who helped the Earl of Lonsdale to judge a Penrith beauty contest; American crooner Bing Crosby on a visit to Greystoke Castle; and a Prime Minister of the future in Harold Wilson whose wife, Mary, once lived in Penrith.

However brief their visits, they were all worthy of note and gave the lustre of stardom and prestige to the news columns.

Thankfully – from the reporters' point of view – royal visits were not frequent. The surrounding bureaucracy and security restrictions made these showpiece occasions hard and frustrating work for the men who recorded them on paper and in pictures. Journalists were virtually shackled to one location, unable to reach the spectators who enjoyed a chat with royalty and might have a story to tell the papers.

HM The Queen made two visits to the area in 1956. Pelting rain hit Appleby when she arrived in the town as part of a tour of Westmorland, although the weather conditions were just part of the problem for the immovable pressmen. A colleague, bereft of interviewing opportunities, reported the name of every identifiable flower in a display on the station platform and, in a further bid to boost his copy, gave a detailed history of the golf umbrella which was used to ensure that Her Majesty was protected from the downpour!

Police on parade. HM Queen Elizabeth inspects a line-up of officers from the Cumberland and Westmorland Constabulary during a visit to Keswick in the 1950s.

I was much luckier in where I was placed. Nearby was a wheelchair-bound woman, Mrs Mary Ousby, a one-time kitchen maid on the staff of King George VI (when he was Duke of York) who had seen Elizabeth as a baby in a cot, thirty years before, and received a piece of the christening cake. Such was the pride in this distant link that Mrs Ousby had had decorations from the cake made up into the brooch she wore as she waited in the downpour.

At Keswick, on a more placid day later in 1956, the young Queen saw the new Lairthwaite School and inspected a centenary parade of the Cumberland and Westmorland Constabulary, although the earlier part of her visit to the county was much more momentous – the opening of the new atomic station at Calder Hall.

Although the *Herald* generally reported the achievements of others, the newspaper had its own share of glory in the fifties when it was featured in *Personal Column*, a programme compiled by the BBC North Home Service. Broadcaster Alfred Hall used an issue of the paper as a mirror of local life and the basis for a series of dips into history and interviews with personalities such as village cricketers, a former wrestling champion, a councillor, a dance band leader and a singing farmer. Long before the days of local radio, *Personal Column* was a considerable accolade to the *Herald* and those who produced it.

CHAPTER 8

A Matter of Principle

I approached the showfield along a narrow country road, walking up the long slope from the village where a service bus had deposited me. It was a gorgeous late summer morning, the hedgerows were ablaze with radiant colour and inquisitive cows clustered just inside the field gates, mooing their welcome. Getting closer to the show, I could hear the sound of music from the Tannoy, punctuated by announcements that the judging of Herdwick sheep was about to start.

With me was Harry from a rival paper. He was an experienced reporter of local repute, whereas I was virtually a new boy, a junior on his first solo show reporting mission. Up to that time I had been to country shows but only as second man to Robert Burne, a journalist who specialized in farming stories and was highly thought of in the local agricultural community. He handled the main reports of shows, but entrusted the slog of collecting results to his junior.

Towards the end of the show season he decided I had absorbed enough to cover one of the smaller events, alone and unaided. I was decidedly nervous because of the weight of responsibility thrust on me, as Harry and I neared the showfield.

On the verge, just outside the open gate, sitting at a small table, were two stewards, cloth-capped sons of the soil. They were armed with rolls of tickets and a cash box.

'Good morning, chaps,' said Harry cheerfully. 'We're press. I'm from Carlisle and John's from Penrith.'

We were about to walk into the field when one of the officials piped up: 'Wait on now. It'll be half a crown apiece.' He thrust out his hand while his companion picked up one of the rolls of tickets.

'No, no,' Harry replied. 'You don't understand. We're from the newspapers. We never pay. We're working.'

'No, *you* don't understand,' the steward insisted. 'You pay today. Everybody pays – the spectators, the committee, the president, *and the press*. It's a new rule here.'

In the space of just half a minute the heat of argument mounted almost to fever-pitch as cash requests were countered by firm refusals. Apprehensive, I let Harry do most of the talking but indicated support with vigorous noddings of the head and appropriate and emphatic 'Of courses' and 'Quite rights'.

We were getting nowhere. 'You had better fetch the show secretary,' said my companion, in the hope that a man of greater seniority would appreciate the justice of our case. Although rather more diplomatic than his bluntly-spoken stewards, the secretary refused to relax the organizers' new rule, which was aimed at boosting dwindling finances.

'Surely you can claim the money back in expenses. Don't tell me your papers cannot afford half a crown apiece,' he argued.

Faced with this impasse, Harry turned on me. 'Come on, John. We cannot accept this – we're going.'

This was a development I had not been prepared for. I was in a state of inner turmoil of doubt and fear as we turned our backs on the resolute show officials and began to walk back towards the village. Should I be doing this? What would my bosses say on Monday morning when I turned up without a report? How would those wise men, Irving and Burne, have handled such an awkward situation?

The sound of the showground Tannoy was fading away. My anxieties continued to mount, despite Harry's words of reassurance, when I became aware of a clunking noise behind us. We were being pursued by a short-panted boy, aged about twelve, whose heavy clogs crunched in the road grit. 'Hey. The man says you two should go back to the show,' he spluttered.

Thank goodness, I thought, envisaging a change of heart by determined officials.

We approached the gate stewards with a feeling of semi-jubilation, only to find that we must still remain in the roadway, as no decision had been taken. The

Sun bathes the picture-postcard showfield just outside the village of Hesket Newmarket; a picture taken early in the 1960s.

Tannoy boomed out an explanation: 'Will all members of the show committee please go to the secretary's tent for a special meeting. At once please, gentlemen. . .'

What had we done? I experienced a tinge of embarrassed guilt at the realization that we had stopped the show. Judging of cattle, sheep and ponies was suspended while officials headed for the emergency meeting. Showgoers clearly wondered what was going on . . . some were gossiping . . . then looking towards the waiting reporters . . .

The emergency meeting lasted only five minutes, though it seemed much longer. The stern-faced secretary, accompanied by two other badge-wearing officials, strode towards the gate.

'Well, the committee have decided by a majority to waive the rule as far as press are concerned and you need not pay to get onto the field,' he told us, adding with some emphasis and, perhaps, a hint of relish, 'but you must pay for your own lunches.'

It was a hollow victory. We had succeeded in defending a long-held principle but it had cost us the customary perk of a free lunch!

Shows varied in their strengths and specialities, some noteworthy for striking line-ups of immaculate Shorthorn cattle while distinctive Swaledale or Herdwick sheep stole the limelight at events closer to the high fells. Immediately after the war some of the showrings were dominated by stately Clydesdale horses, all carefully groomed and glistening with polished brassware. Within a few years they faded almost into oblivion, through tractors taking over most of the heavy work on farms.

We reported the professionally organized Royal and Highland shows when they happened to take place within motoring distance – at, say, Blackpool or Dumfries – but show coverage was mainly local, at Penrith, Appleby, Keswick, Alston, Skelton, Kirkoswald, Ravenstonedale, Brough, Hesket Newmarket and Crosby Ravensworth, among others, plus the county shows of Cumberland and Westmorland.

There was a special feeling of belonging about the smaller shows where the crowds invariably included many former villagers who chose the day to revisit the place of their birth and mingle among old friends. Sometimes it seemed that exhibiting and judging were almost incidental to a massive get-together.

The secretary's tent was the hub of activity. Reporters were generally welcome to base their work in the tent, provided with a table and chairs and given the judges' books, containing the results, as busy stewards brought them in from the cattle ring, the sheep pens and the poultry cages.

Our methods of recording scores of results fascinated, amused and sometimes shocked officials. They never quite understood why the reporters, after being given a couple of copies of the show catalogue, promptly began to rip them apart. This probably seemed an act of needless vandalism but, in fact, there were sound reasons for the disembodiment of the programmes. The separated pages were interleaved to create a thicker, more convenient pad on which the results could be recorded without the necessity of writing on the reverse sides of pages. This simplified and speeded up the recording of results as they were read out from the judges' books, class by class: 'Aged ram, Number 148 is first, 151 second, 146 third'. A colleague marked down the placings against the appropriate numbers – and so on to the next class and the next. It was a time-consuming task which demanded unwavering concentration.

Tan Hill, the highest public house in England, provides the setting for an annual show of Swaledale sheep. This display in 1966 was described by Harry Turner, an auctioneer at Kirkby Stephen, as 'the finest class ever seen'.

The reconstructed catalogues were welcomed by the printers who had an unwritten rule that copy should be written only on one side of the sheets.

Sometimes the solemn exercise of recording results was interrupted (and enlivened) by the discovery that some of the judges' books had gone astray. An errant steward had forgotten to hand them in at the secretary's tent when the judging ended. A loudspeaker announcement often solved the problem but not always. Search parties had to be sent out, generally to the beer tent or the nearest pub, but on several occasions it was found that stewards had dashed home to do the milking, forgetting that the vital books were in the pockets of their overcoats.

Championship-winning exhibitors were interviewed for details of the victorious animals. This could reveal good stories of Swaledale or Herdwick tups which had built up impressive numbers of titles at successive shows, of debutante exhibitors winning at the first attempt, of veteran poultrymen who had been displaying their stocks of hens for fifty or more years and of long-running show rivalries between breeders. The atmosphere in the sheep pens could be electrifying as judges pondered over sturdy rams, their every movement noted by the keen-eyed flockmasters and shepherds leaning over the surrounding woodwork of pens and posts, with pipes going. The first prize might be no more than a tenner but there was much kudos and pride in showing the champion animal in the face of such strong competition.

The settings were visually superb, the officials generally friendly and co-operative and the show lunches tasty and satisfying, but a disconcerting problem common to most country showfields was the inadequacy of toilet facilities. Lengths of hessian nailed to wooden stakes, in some far corner of the arena, hid a makeshift urinal; other needs were not catered for in the days before the introduction of portaloos.

Emergencies could arise, a fact which was brought home to me vividly when I was reporting the show at Brough. I rejected the temptation to use the cover of a nearby hedge and sprinted away into the village, getting to the public toilet in the nick of time and slamming the door behind me. This was a mistake because, as I

Appleby agricultural show in the 1950s. Percy Bishop (left), of Winton, Kirkby Stephen received a top trophy from Thelma Schofield, daughter of the show president, James Schofield. The show has since moved from this setting, on the football field in Chapel Street, to an out-of-town location.

prepared to leave, I found the door was firmly jammed. I was frantic. The highlight of the show, the grand parade, with trophy presentations, was imminent and I was trapped, over half a mile away. The door refused to budge, so I climbed onto the seat and peered out through the tiny window. I was in luck. A herd of cows were being driven past by a sturdy farm worker. Thankfully, he heard my shouts and dashed into the building. 'Stand back,' he yelled. I heard his clogs clattering across the concreted floor outside as he charged the immovable door. There was a dull thud, followed by a string of colourful curses. Two or three more resolute charges had to be made before the door flew open.

I got back to the show in time for the parade, leaving my burly hero nursing a sore shoulder. I offered to help him to pursue his cattle, which had disappeared from sight, but he assured me that they knew their way back to the farm.

Show reporting was demanding, requiring much charging about on large, often muddy fields in search of interviews and information. There was an ambassadorial side to the task because it brought town-based journalists face to face with many countrymen, including characters like George Bowness, the chief steward at Crosby Ravenworth's parish event. George kept the show moving – and the spectators in good mood – with a mixture of wit and dialect: 'Come on lads. Let's be hevin yer Shorthorn coos as sharp as yer can. If yer dun't git a move on, it's gaan t' be neet.'

There is a natural tendency to remember the sunnier days, the pleasanter show officials and the more sumptuous luncheons. Even with that in mind, my memories of country shows, a glass of beer in the secretary's tent, the chatter around the showring and a joke with George Bowness, or one of his style and generation, are more powerful than the occasional clashes with officials or mix-ups over results.

You don't really expect to meet a film star in the middle of a wet field at Threlkeld, a small village in the Lakes. He was an elegant fellow, but warm and friendly and seemed genuinely glad to see me, although it was left to his minder to tell me about his achievements, both on the cinema screen and off. He was the star of *Loyal Heart*, under the name of Fleet, while his minder was Joseph Relph, a Lake District flockmaster, and their normal role was to round up sheep on the high fells. On this occasion, however, they were sharing the limelight as dog and master and competing in the sheepdog trials at Threlkeld's annual 'dog day'. This miscellany of events also included a show of Lakeland foxhounds and terriers and two or three hound trails – the latter a breathtaking sight as the dogs followed the aniseed trail across the face of Blencathra, the mountain overshadowing the village.

My transport to and from the 'dog day' was often a train on the now-extinct Cockermouth, Keswick and Penrith line. On the field I generally met up with a friendly couple, Charlie and Ella Bone, who were reporters in the nearby town of Keswick. On two or three occasions I travelled through to Keswick, staying in their home for a week and writing whatever was to be written while they were away on holiday.

Charlie normally fed us news from Keswick and its surrounding villages but the 'dog day' was deemed to merit coverage by a staff man, as did the other major gatherings of the hunting and sheepdog fraternities, at Patterdale and Rydal. Joe Relph was a modest man but, because of his training of dogs for the films, he was invariably approached for his comments at the trials.

The making of shepherds' crooks and sticks is a traditional Lake District craft. A display of the skill is a feature of the annual 'dog day' at Threlkeld, near Keswick. This picture was taken in 1961, with Tom Nicholson of Greystoke, Penrith, the judge.

The big sales of pedigree Shorthorn cattle, sometimes lasting two or three days, often produced entertainment in the tactics of salesmanship. Many breeders offered generous 'luck money', a payback of a few pounds to the eventual purchaser, but one cunning veteran had an even more tempting offer. As he walked his beast in front of the rostrum he brandished a bottle of whisky as his form of 'luck' – a considerable lure just after the war when spirits were in short supply.

My favourite tactician among the sellers of prime cattle was an ageing farmer who put on his oldest clothes and grimmest expression, creating an impression of abject poverty and, presumably, hoping for sympathetic treatment from auctioneer and bidders. However brisk the bidding was, he was never happy and his upraised stick, under the nose of the auctioneer Jeff Thornborrow, made it clear that the price was far too low to consider. The old man's face was creased in agony and despair. 'He values this one more and is taking her home,' said the auctioneer, but invariably the farmer's stick was dropped at the last second to indicate reluctant acceptance. 'Tha's got a real bargain theer,' shouted the grim-faced veteran as he slouched from the ring.

The auctioneer's banter was laced with familiar clichés: 'There's one to fill the eye' . . . 'We've made a poor start but it's where we finish that matters' . . . 'Try another barrel, Mr H. You can't lose a beast like that for a few pounds' . . . 'He's very disappointed with the price but says he'll have to let her go'.

By far the biggest farming story of the forties and fifties broke in the

Quality cattle come under the hammer. Farmer George Dent looks on attentively from a seat beneath the rostrum, as Penrith auctioneer Jeff Thornborrow sells one of his Shorthorn cattle at a farm sale near Kirkby Stephen, in the Upper Eden Valley.

September of 1957 with the discovery of foot and mouth disease, a rare occurrence, among livestock on six farms in the Penrith district. Within the week, 600 cattle, 1,400 sheep and 340 pigs were slaughtered in a bid to check the disease – and they were just the first to die. The Ministry of Agriculture placed a standstill order on the movement of livestock within a ten mile radius of the farms, and auction marts at Penrith, Lazonby and Appleby were closed. The dreadful scourge of farming communities could not have occurred at a worse time because autumn sales of sheep and cattle, the source of considerable income, were in full swing.

The Ministry set up an office in town, to which I paid frequent visits for progress reports, as the disease spread. Well-known cattle herds were lost under the policy of slaughtering all stock on affected farms, which totalled sixteen before the problem finally subsided.

Over 5,000 animals were killed but, equally serious, the business prosperity of Penrith suffered immeasurably through depleted takings. A firm of farm equipment makers had business cut by two-thirds, a cafe reported losses of seventy-five per cent on market days, the pubs counted their weekly losses in hundreds of pounds. The dependence of Penrith on the farming community was never better illustrated than when it fell under the baleful shadow of foot and mouth disease.

There was court sequel to the unhappy episode when, later in the year, a farmer was fined £50, with £50 costs, for contravening the Foot and Mouth Disease Order by failing to report a diseased pig with practicable speed.

Allowing ponies to stray onto the highway and, occasionally, cruelty to animals were other misdemeanours which led to farmers appearing before the courts. By far the most tempestuous case, however, was that of an elderly farmer who was found to be underpaying his workers – tempestuous because of the reluctance of his workers to give evidence against their boss. They were quite contented, they told the prosecuting solicitor, because, although their income of pounds, shillings and pence might be lower than regulations demanded, the perks of free potatoes, milk, butter and eggs more than compensated for any deficiency. The workers cared little for the strict letter of the law and were angered by the intrusion in their affairs of some Government busybodies, even if it was designed to boost their wage packets.

In my early years Robert Irving sent me to gather news of the biannual ritual of the hiring of farm workers in Penrith's Burrowgate. Twice a year, at Whitsuntide

On clipping day at Harbour Flatt, Murton, near Appleby in 1966, over 1,400 Swaledale sheep were sheared, with one worker still using old-style hand clippers; the rest had more modern equipment. Going back into the last century, farmers joined forces at clipping time; the host providing food and drink. Sometimes the day ended with sports and dancing.

and Martinmas, farm labourers and some female workers went to the hirings in search of new posts, unless they had been invited to 'stop on' by existing employers. They might be hoping to get more pay or a better 'grub shop', as the quality of farmhouse food was a telling factor in losing or retaining a good man.

The farmer wanting to hire labour cast a shrewd eye over the men standing in Penrith. He would move quickly through the crowd, while the unhired lad would stand waiting to be asked. Their eyes would meet and both would be aware that business might be done . . .

The farmer would ask, 'Noo on lad, is tha ta hire an' hoo much is tha assen?'

The lad would name the price for which he was willing to sell his labour for the next half-year, the farmer would bid him two or three pounds less and the bargaining would start.

'Is tha a good milker?' the farmer would inquire.

'Aye, Ah can milk aw reet,' came the reply.

'An is tha a good gitter up?'

There was little hesitation before the reply came: 'Ah dunt think Ah's sa bad that way.'

'An is tha stiddy? Thoo doesn't ga oot and cu back tight or oot like that, does tha?'

This time the reply was more positive: 'No. Ah dunt git any drink, an' if Ah did Ah wadn't be likely to cum in tight varra oft on't wage thoos talking aboot.'

The lad also had a few questions, such as 'Is thine a good meat shop, cos t'last Ah hed was a bad un' and 'Hoo many coos d'yer milk and what time d'yer git finished of a neet?'

After much haggling over the wage, a bargain would be struck. The farmer handed the lad a shilling, according to custom, and the transaction was complete.

From time immemorial, the hiring fairs, with their raucous accompaniment of swings and roundabouts, fat ladies and boxing booths, Aladdin's caves and *What the butler saw* or *The bride's first night* peepshows, were features of the calendar. Travelling cinemas gave Penrith people their first glimpse of the silent movies. The fairs provided a rare taste of urban fun for those who spent most of their lives in rural remoteness.

Hiring fairs are now a fading memory because of the changing character of the agricultural scene in Cumbria. Food production is no longer the overriding objective of land use and, more and more, mechanization and alternative enterprises are taking over from loyal and brawny farm workers.

News columns reflected the multiplicity of activities down on the farm and most aspects of agriculture. There were paragraphs on the starting of the lambing season and on progress with haymaking. Farmers exported prize bulls to New Zealand and Argentina, and stately Clydesdale horses to Canada. Years later, the heavy horses were said to be in decline because of the arrival of tractors. The days of village blacksmiths were numbered.

There were talks in village halls on improving milk yields, debates on the relative merits of Herdwick and Swaledale sheep, meetings to declare 'war' on rabbits, demonstrations on making silage and predictions about the disappearance of smaller farms. Other stories contained results of cereal crop trials and reactions to farm price reviews.

Shepherds' meets, like this one in the hamlet of Dockray, near Ullswater, in the 1960s serve a dual purpose. They enable farmers to sort out any stray sheep, and return them to their rightful owners, and also to enjoy a few drinks, 'tatie-pot' and a singsong in a pub nearby. The Dockray meet is associated with the Royal Hotel.

From time to time the paper featured pictures of sheep clipping days, co-operative efforts when neighbours joined forces to help a farmer to shear his flock. Massive meals were laid on, generally generous slices of cold beef and ham, plenty of pickled beetroot and onions, thickly cut bread and butter and tea. A big barrel of beer was on hand – clipping was thirsty work.

On summer evenings, farm walks drew large crowds to admire pedigree cattle herds and the latest in milk parlours. Dispersal sales of livestock and equipment were also well attended, in the hope of picking up a bargain as well as giving the retiring farmer a good send-off.

Convivial gatherings in the Lakeland fells included shepherds' meets where stray sheep were sorted by means of their markings and returned to their rightful owners. There was a meet of the local foxhounds, followed by a boozy session at the local pub, with big helpings of tatie-pot, traditional songs and other jollification.

The most famous of these occasions was the Mardale meet which was held at the Dun Bull at Mardale before the village was submerged during the 1930s by the building of a dam to turn Haweswater into a reservoir, as a source of water

The Ullswater foxhounds, with huntsman Joe Wear at the head, setting out from Penrith during the 1950s. In the background is the 'Black Angel'; a monument to Penrith men who died in the Boer War, which has since been re-located in the town's park.

supply for Manchester. The Mardale meet lived on in name but with a pub at neighbouring Bampton as the new base.

Towards Christmas another such get-together was the annual shepherds' feast for the men who tended the flocks on Skiddaw. The rafters rang with 'John Peel', 'Joe Bowman' and other hunting songs in the pubs at Bassenthwaite, Caldbeck, Mungrisdale and Threlkeld.

Over the years agricultural reporting has covered almost every kind of field and most parts of the farmyard. Skills like turnip hoeing, hedging, horse ploughing, drystone walling and sheep shearing have all hit farm page headlines. A colleague was once so impressed by the proficiency of a woman shearer that he likened her to a man. Hell hath no fury . . . her letter of complaint ended: 'I have never been mistaken before. Have you ever seen a five feet, four inch man with blonde hair, blue eyes and, dare I say it – yes, breasts?'

CHAPTER 9

A Vital Nuisance

To the raw reporter, column after column of advertisements seemed an obstructive by-product of the industry which caused the omission or delay of vital articles or the harsh editing of some more flowery passages. Manager Robert Burne quickly silenced such complaints: 'Remember that adverts are what pay your wages, lad.'

Press advertising renders a direct service to the general public and to the trading community and, more importantly, it makes possible the sale of papers at low cost to very large numbers of people. In the case of weeklies like the *Herald*, there is a great reader interest in the adverts and notices, ranging from the intimate personal facts of the births, marriages and deaths to the details of bargains in local shops, the announcements of new plans and local government notices and even the situations vacant.

Possibly the most significant adverts in the rich agricultural area served by the *Herald* in the forties were those of the sales of dairy cattle, store lambs and breeding stock at the local marts of Penrith Farmers' and Kidd's, and at Carlisle, Kendal and other Cumbrian centres. Likewise, the paper was studied for guidance (and bargains!) by all wanting dairy nuts or other cattle feed, cattle drench or similar medicines, and any of the vast range of implements and machinery – tractors, drills, harrows, ploughs, balers, milking machines and all the rest.

In my days as a junior, as I watched the make-up of pages, I found compulsive reading in many adverts. Perhaps the overpowering memory is that they were distinctly medicinal and that, whatever your ailment or handicap, you should find some preparation to ease the pain or put you on the road to recovery if you read the *Herald*!

Beaming out of the pages were lovely women whose depression or tiredness had been lifted suddenly thanks to a DCL Vitamin B yeast tablet, or whose inner health had been restored by a dose of Eno's fruit salts. Bonny toddlers, whose thoughtful mums gave them regular spoonfuls of California Syrup of Figs, were the very picture of happiness, while the contentment on the faces of a family of three was attributed to Bisurated Magnesia in preventing stomach upsets. Women wrote testimonies on how Phyllosan kept them fit when over forty.

A small boy, who was apprehensive about a grazed knee, could hasten the healing process with an application of Germolene, and sneezing women were urged to fight off the threats of colds and influenza by taking Phensic, Aspro or

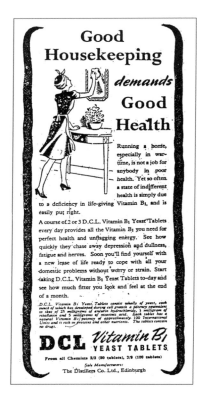

Alasil. You could 'wake up your liver bile' with Carters Little Liver Pills, 'keep youthful looks' with a glass of Limestone Phosphate, get free from rheumatic pains with Kruschen, avoid backaches with Doan's Pills, and relieve aching feet by bathing them in Radox. The list of miracle-makers seemed endless.

Penrith chemist Wilf Swinburn gave a new dimension to the columns by writing dialect verses to promote some of the cures on his shelves:

> Queuing up for rhum may mak yan rheumaticky.
> Ower much geuse or turkey might mak yan stomachy.
> We divn't know a sartin cure for owder,
> But yan can't go far rang wi a Seidlitz powder.

Many 1945 advertisements reflected the continuing war. LMS, LNER, GWR and SR, the predecessors of British Rail, announced proudly that every railwayman was 'redoubling his efforts to give our men the overwhelming weight of arms needed for the final assault on the enemy'.

Another patriotic call came from the Board of Trade, exhorting *Herald* readers to 'Fill the ships and we shall fill the shops'. The plea to export more cars to Australia to pay for more meat imports seemed somewhat out of place in rural Cumberland.

Along came the Ministry of Food with details of how to apply for new ration books or the range of products available with bread units. They even advertised 'brand new recipes' which, supposedly, eked out slender rations or were suitable for wartime products like powdered egg and milk. And as the war neared its end, electricians H.A. Bailey and Son, of Appleby, urged, 'Hear the victory news and celebrations on a new radio, battery or electric.'

The columns reflected keen divisions of opinion, not least as to the best fuel to use in cooking dinner. 'Electric cooking is faster and cheaper, too,' claimed the North Western Electricity Board, but the Northern Gas Board favoured, 'Cooking with positive heat control – the visible flame responding instantly to the turn of a tap'.

Something to drink? The choice was considerable according to the *Herald* over a few weeks – Fry's Cocoa ('The family food drink'), Ovaltine ('The cup that cheers, fortifies and sustains'), Oxo ('Prepared from prime rich beef'), Bovril ('For all-round enjoyment') and Hornimans' Big Dividend Tea (recommended as a means of remaining happily married!). A locally packed brand of tea, from John Parkin Ltd., Appleby, had a unique advertisement in dialect for many years: 'Hy-Cup Tea. It hods oot weel. Sec a laal bit does'.

Likewise, tasty meals seemed guaranteed if people took the advice of one-time advertisers, such as Champion's malt vinegar ('It's best in bottle'), Fray Bentos savoury beef spread ('With the rich, enticing flavour'), Bisto ('Improves all meat dishes'), Burdall's Quicko ('Makes tasty gravy in one minute'), Symington's Vite-Gravy ('How to make a little meat go a long way'), and Pa-Ma Thick sauce, whose makers offered a guinea a time for four-line verses for inclusion in the adverts.

The fashion parade gave the *Herald* of the forties a degree of alluring voluptuousness which seemed strangely at odds with the otherwise chaste columns. While models of the latest styles of women's hats. skirts, suits and summery dresses enlivened the pages, the real eye-catchers were the elegantly coiffured middle-aged ladies who owed their smooth lines to Twilfit, JB, Courtaulds and other manufacturers of girdles, brassieres and suspenders. According to John H. Howe, of The Exchange Warehouse, in Penrith, the secret of figure loveliness was obtainable for 15s 11d, the price of a 'Twilfit girdle with back and side panels of "Wondastretch". Rigid front, fitted with "Lightning" fasteners. Suitable for the petite figure in tea-rose'.

National corset week came but once a year and, with it, came foundation garments for every figure from the teenager to the matron, thanks to Extra-Hi by Silhouette ('Gives you poise, gives you figure confidence') and Playtex girdles ('Magic finger panels give extra tummy support. A miracle-moulding latex to smooth you beautifully').

Tall, handsome men, clearly candidates for top jobs or seats upon boards of directors, strode across the pages in sleek, double-breasted suits and with their

trilby hats at just the right angle. What immaculate buys these gallants could make in a small town. Just after the war, Hepworths of Penrith made men's suits to measure for as little as £6, with overcoats just £5 10s and raincoats a mere £4 15s.

Another corner of the page promised, 'You can be a new man in half-an-hour thanks to the Montague Burton ready-to-wear service'. On a more down-to-earth note, as haytime approached for the farming community, T. Nicholson and Son, of Market Square, Penrith, had all the garments needed for such back-breaking work – kytle jackets and trousers, bib and brace overalls and khaki and navy shirts – with every item at less than £1.

Penrith was the town of the family grocer and, from time to time, the wares of Pattinson and Winter, Pears and Elliott and old Tom Smith were listed. But long gone are the scrubbed wooden floors, the hanging sides of ham, the big cheeses and the upright chairs where farmers' wives rested while going through the ritual of 'the order'. The princes of the provision trade have bowed out to the supermarkets and self-service.

In the pre-television days, when people still queued up outside picture houses to watch James Mason, Margaret Lockwood, Betty Grable, John Wayne, Clark Gable, George Formby and other stars of that era, the cinema notices were avidly read. Fifty years ago the paper's circulation area boasted six such entertainment palaces – Penrith's Alhambra and Regent, Appleby's Cosy, Shap's Gem, a nameless picture house at Kirkby Stephen and Hall's mobile cinema of Morland which transported the delights of Hollywood to villages, like Dufton, Kirkoswald and Crosby Ravensworth. Only the Alhambra survives – and that with several nights devoted to bingo to boost the income.

Another misty memory is of HM Theatre at Carlisle which drew support from across the county and, so, listed its attractions. Perhaps Betty Balfour in the West End success, *Love in a Mist*, or Wheeler and Wilson, radio's sailor and porter, providing 'a laugh a second', with a full supporting cast.

Before television cast its influence on the countryside, social activity prospered in most of the villages and this was reflected in the public notices columns which were crammed with details of leisure pastimes. Whist was exceedingly popular, including military whist drives and those just before Christmas, with geese, chickens and bottles of whisky among the prizes. Dancers of the post-war era foxtrotted and quickstepped to the tones of the Melody Makers, the Rhythm Aces, the Gordonaires and Alan Strong's band.

Among the other convivial get-togethers advertised were concerts, pantomimes, plays, picnics, gramophone recitals and socials. Events with a distinctly agricultural appeal included the farmers' discussion groups ('Cattle at the crossroads' was a popular theme), meetings of the stint holders on local

---

SALVAGE NOTICE.

to the People of PENRITH and Elsewhere.

·———

YOUR BONES

ARE WANTED

Any Bones, old, bones, worn, dog-eaten or dilapidated bones: will make glue, explosives and other vital supplies needed in the War Effort.

———

The lives of our seamen are being endangered and shipping space wasted bringing bones from abroad when we have all the bones we want already in this country, so

SAVE EVERY DISCARDED ANIMAL BONE, HOWEVER SMALL FOR SALVAGE, AND HELP TO WIN THE WAR.

———

Besides BONES the Government want MORE PAPER, BOOKS, RUBBER, RAGS, STRING, etc., and only your SALVAGE can produce these things. If you have any Salvage problem please see or write to the SALVAGE OFFICER at the TOWN HALL, PENRITH.

commons, shepherds' feasts and, moving outdoors, there were sheepdog trials and competitions in the skills of ploughing, turnip hoeing and stock judging.

There were many other events for fund-raising, but also for fun, such as brains trusts, gift sales, fêtes, flower shows, honey shows, swimming galas, autumn fairs, Christmas bazaars, May days and rushbearings. Village life flourished.

Commercial radio and television now pose threats to old-established papers by taking over some of the advertising. However, quality counts and so long as local newspapers of age and standing command the respect and, indeed, the affection of the public, so long will they be the principal medium through which advertising delivers its many messages.

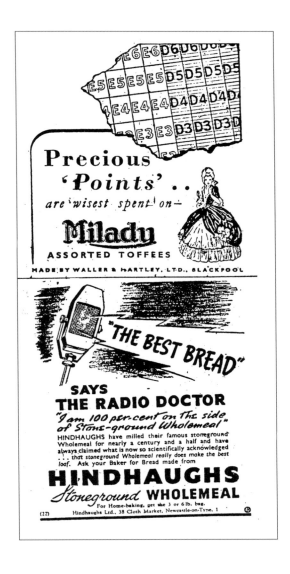

CHAPTER 10

Heroes of the Fellside

Police Sergeant Bob Ivison represented law and order in the village of Shap, plus the spectacular surrounding area, in a manner not unlike that of a sheriff in an old-time movie. In those days the officers in charge of remote districts could not always call in outside support whenever a problem loomed and had to shoulder more responsibility than their counterparts in town and city.

This called for an individuality of style and an ability to make snap decisions on a range of issues, including dealing with minor miscreants, rather than putting them before the courts. But it was the harshness of winters on the A6 over Shap Fell which posed the most demanding tests for Bob Ivison during his many years at Shap. Blizzards swept across the fell road, marooning heavy goods vehicles and drivers in great numbers, and the sergeant was often their guardian, spending long hours in getting men to safety and organizing emergency food supplies and accommodation, sometimes in the village hall at Shap or the police station.

It seemed to the journalists who covered the winter dramas that the tougher the conditions, the more Bob Ivison relished the challenge. I still have a mental picture of him near the fell summit, his greatcoat buttoned to the collar against the whipping snow. He was an indomitable figure.

The jaws of winter bit deep and long on the life of Cumbria (or Cumberland and Westmorland, as it then was). The vilest weather, especially snowstorms, made big headlines in the forties, fifties and sixties: 'Roads blocked and villages cut off . . . Blizzard's return led to more road chaos . . . Doctors lost in raging storm . . . Hungry foxes raid farms . . . Keeping life going in beleaguered villages . . .'.

The majestic mountains and idyllic dales became treacherous and inaccessible during the bitterest depths of winters. In 1962-3 blizzards raged and intense cold descended on the countryside for two full months. Remote communities were completely isolated and at times every main road centring on Penrith became impassable – the A6 over Shap Fell, the A66 over Stainmore, Kirkstone pass on the road leading into Central Lakeland and Hartside pass on the mountainous route to the Pennine-top town of Alston.

Alston Moor itself was likened to the Arctic. In the villages of Nenthead and Garrigill there were pubs with no beer and shops without bread, flour, potatoes, bacon or butter. Flockmaster Johnny Friend Herdman phoned in graphic accounts of the non-stop battle to feed fell sheep and save them from the mounting snowdrifts on the moor.

Stories of hardship, and of initiative in beating extreme conditions, competed

Photographer Robert Armstrong accompanied the helicopter which took relief supplies to Wrenside farm, Kaber; taking this picture as the plane moved in to land. The helmeted figure of the navigator is on the left.

with each other for prominence in the news columns. The anxieties of pregnant women, living in isolated places, led to mercy missions by mountain rescue teams who trudged across snowy wastes with sledges to get the mothers-to-be to safety. Elderly couples were penned in their homes, desperate for more food supplies, and life was tough on dairy farms because the massive drifts prevented both the collection of milk and the delivery of cattle foodstuffs.

The winter of 1963 was the first time helicopters were brought in to airlift supplies to remote farmsteads in the Upper Eden Valley. Photographer Bob Armstrong was allowed aboard for several of these trips and returned with outstanding pictures.

While the snowfall seemed almost nonstop, the severity of the winds contributed largely to the chaos of the road closures, piling up gigantic drifts. I made daily calls to a Civil Aviation weather station, 2,800 ft above sea level on the summit of Great Dun Fell, in the Pennines, where wind speeds were recorded, sometimes well over 100 mph.

Farmers, visiting Penrith for the weekly auction mart, crowded into Dayson's coffee shop and complained about 'the lazy wind' outside – 'ower lazy to blaw roond thee, so it gaes reet through'.

An icy blast unique to the East Fellside and the Eden Valley is the Helm wind which is signified to those further away by a distinctive wedge of cloud, the Helm bar, hanging ominously over the Northern Pennines. In years past the *Herald* carried many stories about its ferocity, one of the more extreme suggesting that

At the height of the blizzards of 1963, RAF helicopters were called in to airlift much needed cattle foodstuffs, fuel oil and groceries to remote farms. The supplies were put aboard at the Kirkby Stephen depot of Cumberland and Westmorland Farmers Ltd.

One of the helicopter crew delivers welcome supplies to the farmer of Wrenside, Kaber, Fred Ellwood, accompanied by his wife and daughter Pauline.

growing turnips were torn out of a farmer's field. While I never came across an experience quite so sensational, I was once assured that a cricket match was cancelled at Gamblesby, at the foot of the Pennines, because the Helm knocked the stumps out of the pitch.

So prolonged was the big freeze of 1963 that the ice on Ullswater became solid enough for motorists to drive their cars across. Pupils of a private school even built and lit a substantial bonfire on the ice-covered lake surface. On a more serious note, the lake swans, which normally fed near Howtown, were threatened by the intense cold until a local 'Lady Bountiful' emerged in the person of Viscountess Lowther, the mother of the Earl of Lonsdale, who begged bread from the bakeries to feed the hungry birds.

The most disastrous sequel of the freeze-up of 1963 was the loss to Penrith of its main social centre, the Drill Hall, which was struck by a night fire. In ordinary circumstances, the outbreak would have been dealt with but, because of the severe frost, the mains water supply had been turned off overnight. What water there was in fire service tenders quickly ran out and, in the ensuing state of panic, over an hour elapsed before the main supply became available, enabling the blaze to gain a firmer hold. A controversial decision to demolish the fire-damaged building was rued for years afterwards.

If Penrith people were saddened to hear of the old hall being pulled down, they were shocked to turn the corner and see workmen building a new block. The notice said, 'New Crown Office. A Pilot Metric Project'.

How could they metricate memories? And why the local headquarters of the Inland Revenue as a replacement for a place once associated with grand balls, handsome men, elegant women, swirling silk, sophisticated perfumes and blossoming romance?

Even those of a later generation could look back on the post-war glory years of the Drill Hall, especially the Saturday night dances–the 'bob hops' –when we waltzed and quickstepped to the mellow tones of Frank Walton and his Melody Makers. Frank was the town's Glenn Miller, playing everything from the harmonious 'In the mood' or 'Who's taking you home tonight?' to the more raucous gaiety of 'Waiting for the Robert E. Lee' or 'I've got a lovely bunch of coconuts'. A golden age of community spirit and vibrant enjoyment was ended sadly and suddenly by a deadly combination of fire and plunging temperatures–and a failure to replace what had been lost!

Rightly or wrongly, I associate the disappearance of the Drill Hall with the fading away of the togetherness of the town. It appeared to mark the start of a gradual break-up of the heyday of post-war Penrith. There were aiding and abetting factors in the advent of television, the greater availability of motor cars and the shutdown of some of the chummy pubs. Or perhaps I was simply getting older. . . .

Brough Hill, a ragged-looking stretch of ground alongside the A66 in the Upper Eden Valley, once drew thousands of gypsies on the last day of September and the first of October, when the roar of passing traffic was challenged by the cries of cheapjacks and the clatter of the hooves as ponies and horses were put through their paces. Unlike a similar gathering of gypsy folk at nearby Appleby – which continues to attract vast crowds, in midsummer – Brough Hill fair has gone into sharp decline

A picture from 1965 showing the age-old horse fair held each June just outside the town of Appleby. The fair survived several closure attempts by the local authorities, mainly on the grounds that it was considered insanitary. The layout of caravans has been altered since this picture was taken.

in recent years. But whatever its eventual fate, it will never be forgotten because 'Brough Hill weather' has become part of the local vocabulary as a graphic description of the worst of wind, rain and snow – conditions which have regularly prevailed during the once-boisterous get-togethers, now reduced to a state of lingering death and attended by only a dozen or so caravans.

The vagaries of the Cumbrian weather were illustrated by a freak snowstorm which hit the East Fellside one mid-June. Fred Horrobin, a local photographer, not only got a shot of two schoolboys engaged in a snowball fight, but returned to the village school precisely a week later, during a heatwave, to picture the same lads enjoying ice-cream cones.

It is in foul weather that people get lost, injured and killed on the mountains, although there are many other factors, such as the dubious health and the fecklessness of some folk on the high fells. Exertions can cause heart attacks and other fatal collapses. Many walkers set out in inadequate clothing and without maps or compasses; one woman was found high in the mountains on a wintry day wearing fashion boots and a mini-skirt.

Late one evening in the fifties Bob Armstrong took me out to the fellside village of Murton, a few mile from Appleby. A party of schoolchildren had just arrived back there to find that one of their number, a teenage girl, had become separated from the group; she was missing somewhere in the fells as darkness descended. Under the leadership of Squadron Leader Lester Davies, the warden of the Ullswater Outward Bound School, the rescue service mounted an operation with impressive speed and efficiency. By first light the next day the normally placid little village was buzzing with activity, as rescue teams gathered and the WVS set up a refreshment point to sustain the troops before they set out. On that occasion the missing girl turned up, unhurt, at Middleton-in-Teesdale, some miles away, but the slickness of the voluntary effort brought home to me the value of the service being provided by mountain rescue teams. They were bound to be in ever-growing demand with the increase in popularity of fell walking as a leisure activity.

Many people assume that these rescuers are publicly funded. The fact is that they are all volunteers and also have to raise most of the cash needed to fund the vital service. Outsiders are not aware of the sacrifice of time and money of the team members. It is ludicrous that men and women who comb the fells, searching for missing walkers and rescuing people with heart attacks and broken limbs, should have to rely for cash on sponsored walks, slide shows, collecting tins and local generosity.

This was the scene of wreckage and devastation which awaited police, rescue teams and press photographers in October 1961 when they climbed 2,000 feet up Croglin Fell, in the Cumbrian Pennines, to investigate a crash involving a Dakota airliner, en route from Leeds to Carlisle. The crew of four were killed.

CHAPTER 11

Men of Action

The reporter's story can be written after the event but the news picture can only be captured by the photographer being in the right spot at the right time.

The news editor must deploy the photographic forces to the best possible effect. Sometimes, however, the demands are such that papers like the *Herald*, with only one full-time cameraman available, face problems in drawing up a list of assignments.

Open the office diary on a day around the height of summer and you will appreciate how conflicting demands can be the bane of life of the country newspaperman, as he attempts to keep everybody happy in commissioning pictures.

Organizers cannot appreciate the effect of a clash of assignments and, naturally, see their own event as the most important. There is no doubt that many functions merit pictorial coverage; the big question is whether the paper's only photographer can perform the miracle of getting to all the places involved, as they are frequently many miles apart.

There are days when the photographer needs the high-speed driving skills of a Stirling Moss or a Damon Hill and the endurability of a marathon runner. His day is not finished when he takes the last pictures; he must get back to his studio and turn out the prints which have to be on the news editor's desk by 8.30 the next morning.

A feature of the *Herald* over many post-war years was a weekly front page picture, over three or four columns, showing a Lake District beauty spot, a leafy glade, a picturesque pub, a lake steamer, a blacksmith or a ploughman at work, anglers beside a stream or a meeting of one of the Lakeland foxhound packs. Irreverently known as 'pretty-pretties', these pictures were taken by Joseph Hardman, a Kendal man who travelled around the area in a hire-car, a distinctive rather portly figure who used an old-style tripod and plate camera. He was often accompanied by his attractive daughter who sometimes figured in the pictures, masquerading as a hiker, a sunbather or a picnicker.

The newsier pictorial content has generally been the work of a series of Penrith-based photographers. Eric Davidson, Alec Fraser, Robert Armstrong and Fred Wilson have also been 'ambassadors' of the paper in giving a good service over the far-flung circulation area.

Eric was a legendary figure among the reporters of his day and generation. They competed with each other in telling tales of his exploits; the older ones still do.

When taking indoor pictures of groups he used a flash gun which incorporated what can only be described as a large dustbin lid, held independently and directed downwards at the top table diners, the beauty queens or whoever was having their picture taken. Local folk became accustomed to this peculiar device being brandished above their heads – sometimes by Eric, sometimes by a kindly volunteer – but it was a mirth provoking experience for the uninitiated. Staid men found it difficult to keep a straight face; more alarmingly, the dustbin lid once 'exploded', showering the company with glass.

Eric possessed engineering skills and had worked for Rolls Royce during the war. One of his unfulfilled ambitions was to build a mobile dark-room to speed up the production of photographic prints. With a burly German names Hans, a former prisoner of war who worked as his assistant, he attempted to convert an old car for this purpose, and welded on a number of steel plates. Alas, the plating was so heavy that the car became almost immovable and the idea foundered. Eric was the 'character' of the post-war picture men and told hilarious tales, often at his own expense.

Alec Fraser, originally a driver of heavy goods vehicles and buses, entered the world of newspaper and commercial photography in his middle years, and was ultra-reliable with a keen eye for a good shot. Long after his retirement he gave hundreds of old pictures to the *Herald*, who used them each week as part of a popular 'heirlooms' series.

Robert Armstrong began his working life as a shop assistant. Photography was a hobby which became a full-time job when he turned freelance, working for the *Penrith Observer,* the *Herald* and any other papers needing pictures.

Bob Armstrong was a workaholic – perhaps 'newsaholic' is a better word. Whatever the hour, day or night, he turned out willingly, even zestfully, if he got a tip-off on a hard news story. His heavy boots were in the car boot in case he was called on to walk up to a mountain to an aeroplane crash, and he took his chance on flooded or snow-covered roads if he thought they would lead him to spectacular pictures. During the blizzards of 1963 he 'cadged' lifts on the helicopters which took relief supplies to remote farms marooned by massive snowdrifts.

After a long day covering a football match at High Wycombe – Penrith had been playing there in a cup-tie – Bob was driving home through the night. As he neared Penrith, around 11 o'clock in the evening, the car radio picked up a police message about a serious accident at Penruddock, between Penrith and Keswick. A car had crashed through a bridge wall and landed on the railway line, trapping the driver and his girl passenger. More overtime became essential; covering the drama added another three and a half hours to Bob's working day.

The fire brigade passed on the word that they had been summoned to a local quarry to rescue a young man who had lost his nerve when climbing down a rockface and was afraid to move, either up or down. Because of the climber's perilous plight, a friend at the foot of the ascent was shouting out the latest scores in a Test match, taken from a radio commentary, in the hope of taking his mind off the danger he was in.

As we drove to the quarry, an officious policeman barked out an order that we should wait outside until the firemen got the climber to safety. Feigning deafness,

Bob yelled back 'What do you say?' and drove on to get some dramatic shots of the rescue operation.

He eventually moved from weekly journalism to the heady world of filming the news for the BBC in Newcastle, although he continued to live in Penrith and kept in touch with old friends and colleagues. Sadly, he died suddenly when still at the peak of his career. Taking pictures for weekly newspapers in rural districts is not for the faint of heart. Eric, Alec and Bob all bought back some wonderful photographs; more importantly, perhaps, they were welcome representatives of the paper in distant corners of the widespread circulation area, as is their present-day successor, Fred Wilson.

CHAPTER 12

Campaign to Save a Lake

Newspapers champion the causes closest to them, as well as reporting upon them. The *Herald* files are dotted with campaigns in which the newspaper itself has figured prominently among the standard-bearers. Down the years, the editors have been motivated to write with feeling, frequency, but with varying degrees of effect, on countless emotive issues – the threatened closure of the Settle–Carlisle railway line, the failure to bypass the accident-prone village of Temple Sowerby on the A66, the persistent danger of Appleby's picture-postcard cricket field being lost to the house builders, and the obnoxious 'pong' emanating from an offal-processing plant to the great discomfiture of the people of Penrith.

By far the greatest of the *Herald*-inspired campaigns, led by editor George Hobley, was the fight to save Ullswater from the water engineers of Manchester Corporation when, in 1961–2, they sought Parliamentary powers to obtain further sources of supply in the Lake District. Over six months, with mounting zeal, the *Herald* highlighted the proposal and the threat it posed to natural beauty.

There was opposition, too, from the enthusiasts of the Ullswater Preservation Society and the Friends of the Lake District but it was George Hobley, probably more than any other individual or any public body, who galvanized the local community, and others much further afield, to join in the battle, either by writing protests or signing petition forms:

Manchester Corporation's proposals for abstracting water from Ullswater can best be defeated by the weight of public opinion, but to thwart the designs of the city on England's fairest lake it is essential that the opposition should be concerted and strengthened. . . . As a sterile reservoir, Ullswater would be no use to anyone except the thirsty people of Manchester.

To the ordinary person it is simply unbelievable that in the twentieth century, with all its engineering achievements, the need for more water in Manchester or anywhere else cannot be met without invading England's most beautiful lake

Perhaps we in this office, the *Herald*, are in a better position than most to judge the strength of the feeling aroused because, in addition to hundreds of callers to sign the petition and letters asking for forms, there has been a stream of contributions on the subject – poems and articles, newspaper cuttings and books – so numerous as to make publication, or even mention of them all, quite impossible.

The Herald *played a leading role in a campaign to oppose Manchester Corporation's 1961 bid for Parliamentary powers to extract water from Ullswater. Behind-the-scenes workers (above) despatched petition forms to many parts of Great Britain and some to foreign lands; they were led by retired Tyneside businessman Thomas Smith (standing, centre).*

George Hobley's pen produced virtually all the copy on the water extraction plan, both the week-by-week reports and the editorial comment. The word 'pen' is used deliberately because, like others of his time, he never used a typewriter.

Feelings ran high, as was evident from the number of protests contained in the editor's mailbag. There was a world-wide response to the call for signatures on petition forms, an exercise which was largely organized by a retired Newcastle industrialist, and lover of Ullswater, Thomas Smith. Another volunteer, Mrs C.M. Phillips, of Harrogate (and formerly of Penrith) gathered 3,000 signatures single-handed. Masses of signed petitions arrived from the USA, Canada, Spain, Italy, Hong Kong and Singapore.

What was initiated as purely local opposition to the Manchester 'invasion' spread to the national press. The *Daily Telegraph* columnist, Peter Simple, represented the views of more ardent campaigners when he wrote:

This Bill ought to be resisted to the last ditch. If I recommended armed resistance, I should, I suppose, be contravening the law; so I will not do so. But here is a cause, not vague and unpractical like 'Ban the bomb' but local and precise, a cause for which a passive resistance campaign could really achieve something.

Myself, I am ready to sit down on the banks of Ullswater for months on end, if necessary. And even if nobody else will sit with me, I shall know that the great shades of Wordsworth and Coleridge, Ruskin and Arnold are at my side.

In recognition of the notable part played by Lord Birkett in the defeat of Manchester Corporation's plans to use Ullswater as a water supply, a nearby fell was named after him in 1962. Boys and instructors from Ullswater Outward Bound School, led by the warden, Squadron Leader Lester Davies, built a cairn with a commemorative tablet.

After the intensive barrage of words directed against Manchester, it was left to the House of Lords, and, in particular, Lord Birkett of Ulverston to deliver the finishing blow when, by 70 votes to 36, the waterworks clauses relating to Ullswater were deleted from the Manchester Corporation Bill, following a debate of eloquence and passion lasting seven and a half hours. Lord Birkett, in opposing the second reading of the Bill, pleaded that Ullswater should not suffer the same fate as Thirlmere and Haweswater – 'both lovely lakes which have now been murdered . . . now dead reservoirs, with no human life and sterile shores'.

The great advocate crowned his career – in fact, ended his career – with his successful defence of the natural beauty of Ullswater. On the following day he was taken ill and underwent an emergency operation in the London Clinic and twenty-four hours later, just two days after his final triumph, he died at the age of seventy-eight.

Almost exactly two years after the defeat of their first attempt to tap Ullswater, Manchester Corporation returned to the fray with new plans, showing important changes which, according to a *Herald* headline rendered the abstraction 'unseen and unheard', with water pumped under the dividing fells to Haweswater, seven miles away.

The fact that, under the new scheme, the city got its water but that every effort was made to ensure that the lake did not lose its natural beauty and charm, had much to do with the protest of 1961-2, not least the part played by the *Herald* and its campaigning editor.

CHAPTER 13
Political Passions

Television's current domination of parliamentary elections had not even dawned when the country went to the polls in 1945. Political passions pulsated, even in remote places, and people were still motivated to crowd into public halls and school buildings to applaud and to heckle, to listen to oratory and to voice fears and concerns.

Election campaigns were demanding times in rural areas, such as the divisions of Westmorland and neighbouring Penrith and Cockermouth. Each weekday evening the candidates set out to address five or six neighbouring communities, preceded along the road by party officials and other vocal supporters who 'warmed up' audiences until the main speakers arrived.

As candidates' speeches rarely varied in content, we, as reporters, relied heavily on the ensuing question and answer sessions to provide more lively copy. Questions covered a wide range of topics in 1945 when the Beveridge report was under discussion – there was concern about future relationships with our wartime allies, Russia and America – and the old age pension seemed scandalously low.

Newspapers were more integral to the democratic system half a century ago than was later to be the case. Their co-operation was essential in almost every aspect of government. From the House of Commons to small parish councils, newspapers were the link and the liaison between public bodies and the people who elected them. With few political broadcasts over the airwaves in 1945, it was through the papers that MPs and, at election time, candidates made their views known.

The *Herald*'s policy was both responsible and exhausting: as far as was possible, we carried photographs and pen-pictures of each candidate when nominations closed, and reported their meetings twice a week up to polling day. Our attempts were sometimes frustrated, with too few questions to test the candidates or to provide lively copy, although I got an early taste of political fervour and excitement in the form of a visit to Alston Moor, as assistant to Robert Burne.

Three of the four Penrith and Cockermouth contenders were due to address meetings and could be covered in the space of a single evening. The resultant story filled most of a page, under the heading of 'Political drums beat on Alston Moor' – and if that suggested war drums, it was highly appropriate! Five meetings were reported, the most spirited by far being in Alston Town Hall

Councillors in session. Penrith Urban Council administered the town until the local government reorganization in 1974 when Eden District Council was formed, embracing five smaller authorities. W. Denis Burns was the chairman at this meeting, with Town Clerk Herbert Rayworth alongside him.

where the Conservative candidate, Colonel Alan Dower, faced a barrage of heckling from an audience of nearly 300. My senior colleague's shorthand captured the sensation of animosity which pervaded the evening:

Questioner – During any of the five years before 1940 did you ever put in above 50 per cent attendances, as shown by the divisions in which you voted?

Colonel Dower – You interest me because you talk such unutterable rubbish. In 1937 when you were being pushed in your pram . . .

Questioner – I joined the Air Force in 1939. Not so much about being pushed in your pram in 1937.

Colonel Dower – Surely you were in your pram in 1937 (Uproar).

Questioner – You still have not answered my question.

Colonel Dower – You want the whole evening . . .

Questioner – How many times were you in this constituency between 1935 and 1939?

The Chairman – Are there any more intelligent questions, please?

Another questioner – Yes. Why did Colonel Dower not support Churchill until the present time?

Colonel Dower – Don't believe him. I have been a greater supporter of Churchill than he has been.

The exchanges were both fast and furious. Robert Burne's pen flashed across the notebook page, not missing a word. 'This is good stuff,' he muttered without checking his note-taking for a split second.

Seldom, if ever, in covering general elections over the years, did I experience a meeting as full-blooded and angry as that Alston battle of words. The candidate was still fending off questions when the Chairman suddenly announced the meeting was closed. Unusually, there was no vote of thanks to the speakers.

Commotion spilled over into the cobbled street outside the Town Hall, as attempts to drive away Colonel Dower's car were foiled by political opponents barring his path by parking their vehicles, to the accompaniment of mirthful jeering. The obstructive tactics continued until the police were called to clear the road.

A couple of weeks later, I was entrusted to describe eve of poll activity in Penrith. The piece was to be descriptive, rather than a record of speechifying, as voting was to take place before the next issue was printed. My six-hour task began in early evening when Tom Mitchell, an Independent from West Cumberland and favourite of local farmers, addressed an open-air meeting in Corn Market. Excitement was sustained until midnight when Liberal Noel Newsome spoke to the masses from the flat top of a wartime air raid shelter and, in the throes of his peroration, seemed dangerously close to falling off. By that hour the hecklers were in playful mood; at a time when the national agenda was packed with more serious considerations, Noel Newsome spent an unwarranted amount of time on the desirability of Penrith cinemas opening on Sundays.

As at Alston, the barrackers concentrated their anger on the Conservative candidate and his supporters but, despite the disturbances which dotted his meetings, Colonel Dower was to emerge triumphant with a majority of over 2,000 over the Liberal.

Another new experience, that of attending the election count, proved surprisingly disappointing. So strict were the rules and regulations that I found myself virtually shackled to the seat I was allocated at the back of the hall. Although it was impossible to see how the rival contenders were faring, I was sternly warned that I must not go close to the curtained windows, as this could be interpreted as an attempt to signal news of the count to the crowd in the street outside – a ridiculous suggestion because there was no way I could possibly have known. (Contrast this with the easy-going attitudes of later years when television cameras were admitted to the counts).

Late in 1951 a middle-aged, flat-capped, rather timid man walked into the reporters' room. He might well have been bringing in a report of a chapel anniversary or a whist drive. In fact, he announced: 'I thought I should let you know that I'm standing as a candidate in the election.'

William Brownrigg, from Kirkbampton, Carlisle, was quite the most unconventional would-be politician I ever encountered. Having just handed in his nomination papers in the nick of time, he strolled down from the Town Hall to let

A solemn moment. The traditional Mayor-making ceremony in the Moot Hall at Appleby, as Councillor Frank Betts (right) is installed as Mayor of the borough. Addressing him is Alderman James F. Whitehead, with Town Clerk Tom Longstaff on the left.

the paper know of his ambitions and his offbeat manifesto, written on a single sheet of notepaper. This was a wide-ranging document, as farmer Brownrigg's aims included:

New factories to be free of rates for 12 years.
National Insurance to be voluntary.
Cockfighting to be legalized.
Sweepstakes to be legalized, as in Ireland.
Foxhunting to remain.
Lower rate of tax for admission to horse racing.
Potatoes from Scotland to be labelled 'as with Irish'.
'Monte Carlo' to be allowed in Cumberland.

Mr Brownrigg told colleague George Hobley that he would expand on this 'policy' when he visited the local auction mart to speak to farmers. 'Follow him and see what he has to say,' I was instructed. The surprise candidate merely engaged in conversation with one or two men he saw in the street leading to the railway station, before catching his train back to Carlisle.

Although he polled only 158 votes, William Brownrigg stood again at the following election when he again failed, this time behind the emergent William Whitelaw, later to hold high government offices, including that of Home Secretary, and to become Viscount Whitelaw. On this occasion, the veteran farmer more than doubled his vote after advocating better pay for mole catchers and home rule for Cumberland, with the county minting its own currency!

Men like William Brownrigg do not enter the political arena very often but the memories of them are more lasting than those of more successful opponents.

Years after his election defeats, he claimed that they did not cost him a penny because he accepted sufficient wagers to cover the expenditure involved. Friends offered him odds of 50-1 that he would not dare to stand as a candidate.

Politics never featured in local government in my early years with the *Herald*. At general election time most of the sixteen members of Penrith urban council probably voted Liberal or Conservative, although that can only be a surmise because within the council chamber there was seldom a hint as to who they supported politically. Local councillors all claimed to be 'independent' – and many still do.

Local government matters figured prominently in the paper. Their significance was always stressed by Robert Irving because, among other public duties, he was a long-serving urban councillor, with a special interest in finance. He was the local 'chancellor of the exchequer' and his annual budget statement, prior to the fixing of the rate for the next financial year, was always front page news.

Councillors tended to have their special interests and pet hates. Isaac Sim devoted much of his career on the council to the provision of houses and spoke with authority on the development of council estates. If Laurie Harker, a retired farmer, rose to his feet, the reporters knew he was probably about to lambast lazy gardeners for neglecting to attend to their council-owned allotments. Fred Lunson, a garage owner, seldom failed to warn of some terrible fate awaiting dog owners who allowed their pets to foul the streets.

Over those early post-war years the local councils had several 'rebels' or 'firebrands' and I use those words in tribute, rather than criticism. Cliques and collusions there were bound to be on local authorities but the 'rebels' remained apart and aloof, probing, questioning and frequently, it seemed to me, more aware of the concerns of the ratepayers. They could shine light in darkened corners and put meat on the bones of brief reports.

J. Simpson Yeates resisted costly schemes to justify his election-time clarion call of 'Vote for Yeates and keep down the rates', but the most fiery of Penrith's post-war councillors was J.J. Moffat, known locally as 'Cherry Blossom', the brand of shoe polish he sold as a commercial traveller. A distinctive figure with a shock of white hair protruding from beneath his bowler hat, he arrived at meetings with a fistful of sheets of paper, his speeches for the evening ahead. Scathing comments from colleagues did not deter him. He lost his fight to retain *Hansard*, the daily record of happenings in the House of Commons, in the town library, but defeated a move to introduce professional boxing into a building owned by the council.

Sometimes Mr Moffat's word-power did not quite match his vehemence and at other times he overstepped the mark in his condemnations. He was ruled out of order and ordered to sit down by indignant chairmen but was resilient to criticisms and quickly re-entered the fray, brandishing his bunch of papers.

Of the same ilk, though slightly more restrained, Geoffrey Johnston caused annoyance and took up precious time as he posed his questions. What mattered was that he prompted others to give more thought to issues which might otherwise have been passed 'on the nod' without adequate debate and without the public being made fully aware of what was going on. The old urban district council was remarkably non-political but Geoff Johnston could provide an opposition, single-handed.

Among the most single-minded of councillors was Jack Varty, dubbed 'Mr Penrith' because the town had no greater champion. In a quarter of a century, first on the urban council and then, after local government reorganization, on Eden district council, he was at his most eloquent and effective when pleading for Penrith. In particular, he fought for the preservation of the essential character of the old town, opposing the conversion of town centre shops into offices, and resisting housing development in sensitive areas like Beacon Edge.

Another councillor with a mission was Harry Noble, a grizzled veteran on Penrith rural council, for whom the supply of electricity to his village, Ousby, was almost all that mattered. Whatever the theme of a discussion, or however

Penrith Urban Council chairman Kenneth Jones gave an official welcome to Ena Sharples, the gossip-mongering busybody of Coronation Street, *the TV soap opera. However, the 1961 'visit' was a complete hoax, designed to draw attention to a Penrith YMCA flag day. Colin Jackson, aged eighteen, played the part of Mrs Sharples.*

deserving a new council project, Harry could somehow make the point that the provision of power to the East Fellside community was much more essential. Harry never won recognition in the honours list – but Ousby eventually got its electricity.

Local government coverage was — and is still — vital to the *Herald* because of its great concern to the readership (though sometimes one got the impression that everybody was happy so long as their dustbins were emptied each week).

Over the post-war years there have been several moves to tamper with the structure of local government. In 1973-4 new district authorities took over from the hosts of small urban and rural councils which had run the towns and country areas since 1894. This reorganization saw the former Penrith urban and rural, Appleby borough, North Westmorland rural and Alston-with-Garrigill rural supplanted by a new Eden district council, with its headquarters in Penrith. This was seen as a means of slimming down staff numbers, slashing costs and stepping up efficiency. Nobody could now convince the ratepayers that these ambitions were fully achieved.

A further maelstrom of doubt descended on the area in 1993-4. The existing two-tier system, with district councils working alongside a county council, which had responsibility for highways, the police, education and social services, was considered untidy and confusing. Local government commissioners plugged a switch to a new structure whereby Cumbria would be divided into two big unitary authorities which would provide all the services. The alarm bells rang in remote hamlets where the people feared that local democracy was under threat. A strange sense of disbelief, even outrage, engulfed rural Cumbria at the prospect of unwieldy areas, tinkering with the boundaries and loss of identity by places which were happy with their locally based authorities.

The fear was that local was to be removed from local government. The ghosts of J.J. Moffat, Geoff Johnston and Jack Varty would surely have stalked the corridors of Penrith Town Hall had this change not been fended off – at least for the time being.

A disquieting cloud hovering over the local government scene was the tendency towards undue secrecy, with the reporters excluded from the start or asked to leave meetings for certain debates. Communities could be deprived of information about exciting projects, sometimes great news which should have been shouted from the rooftops, rather than shrouded in secrecy, awaiting some mysterious rubber-stamping before being released. Items of obvious interest, ranging from major planning controversies to the granting of government cash to transform old property – even lighthearted discussions about some aspect of the Hypnotism Act – have been deemed to merit great seclusion. Reporters were told to leave council meetings because the debates might lead to 'the likely disclosure of exempt information as defined by paragraph 4 of part 1 of schedule 12A of the Local Government Act'.

Some of these dismissals caused reporters to seethe with indignation. The suspicion was that councillors chose to retreat into privacy as a means of protection, as they did not want ratepayers to learn of what they said or how they voted on disagreeable matters.

Although council activities and decision-taking fill many columns in newspapers like the *Herald*, there is a persistent cloud of public apathy where local government is concerned. To be fair, the nitty-gritty of rates, rents, street cleansing, dustbin emptying and granting taxi licences is unlikely to whip up much interest or bring younger people surging into council chambers with a freshness of approach.

While there are veteran councillors with proud records of membership stretching back over thirty years, local government is less favoured as a form of public service than, say, the Lions, Rotary and Round Table clubs which have the added attraction of a strong socializing element. There is a grave danger of many local authorities becoming old men's clubs. Through covering the many aspects of local government, newspapermen can generally assess the worthiness, the strengths and the weaknesses of individual councillors. Most of them would not offer themselves for election if they were not men and women of commitment, prepared to make some personal sacrifice to sit through long, sometimes boring meetings and to help individual ratepayers with their problems in a behind-the-scenes way.

Councillors vary in their willingness to give up their time and in their effectiveness. Some use strong, often unkind words in the heat of the debate, but better an outspoken councillor than one who is reluctant to enter into discussion on a tricky topic. Whatever their type, few councillors deserve all the criticism they get, especially as some of the most scornful comments are directed at them by the very people who shun the responsibility for local government or, indeed, for any form of community service.

CHAPTER 14

The Murder of a Manager

The young man who walked into a bank in a small town was unknown to casual onlookers . . . a minute or so later the bank's alarm bell rang out, followed a split second later by the crack of a pistol shot . . . the stranger dashed from the bank, jumped into a car that was parked nearby and drove off at high speed, narrowly avoiding a collision as he headed out of town.

This was the essence of a phone call which Robert Irving was taking from the paper's part-time correspondent at Alston, when I got back into the office just after lunch. The fuller facts, which were to emerge on that unforgettable September day in 1949, were that Andrew Steele, the sixty-year-old manager of a branch of Midland Bank, situated in the sloping main street of Alston, had been mortally wounded, shot by a young man who entered the building, supposedly to open a new account. But he then demanded money and when the manager pressed an alarm button the robber shot him and ran from the building. A colleague dashed into the manager's office. Andrew Steele gasped: 'He shot me. I'm dying.' A doctor was called but there was no hope of saving the wounded man. 'I did not surrender,' he said repeatedly. Mr Steele died later in the day in the Cumberland Infirmary, in Carlisle.

Ten minutes after the alerting call, I was heading out of Penrith to the scene of the crime alongside senior colleague Robert Burne. It was a chilling experience because I realized that, as we drove over the winding moorland road of the Hartside pass, we might well encounter the fleeing man, who was armed with a pistol. And so it proved, though not quite as I feared.

In fact, we had not reached the mountain pass when we saw ahead of us two motor patrol policemen standing beside a stationary car. Inside, slumped behind the steering wheel, was the wanted man, twenty-four-year-old Charles Kennedy. The thwarted bank robber had turned the gun on himself.

The full story of that tragic day was still unravelling, for the car was not Kennedy's but had been hired much earlier in the day from a garage in Durham and was driven as it left there by Ernest Ingram. On the way to Alston, Ingram was shot dead and his body was found in a ditch near Stanhope, covered with stones.

When Robert Burne and I got to Alston, a town full of shock and sorrow but buzzing with the excitement of it all, it soon became known that we had chanced across the dead bank raider on our way there. People wanted to talk to us as much as we did to them.

I interviewed the owner of an ice-cream parlour, opposite the bank, and a teenage shop assistant, Ailsa Spark, who gave me a graphic account of events: 'I heard the alarm and, at the same time, the firing of a shot. A second or so later the man came out of the bank and, half-running, half-walking, crossed the street to where the car was parked. I don't know whether he had left the engine running but his getaway was so fast that I think he must have done. He simply flew away.'

I have always admired Robert Burne's report of the crime, made up of short, pithy sentences. No excessive verbiage was needed; the facts were so dramatic and gripping that fine words would have been superfluous. My contribution ran alongside the main report – a column on the interviews with the ice-cream parlour women and other onlookers, headed 'Alston eye-witness accounts: gunman's getaway described'.

There were to be several postscripts to the story of the foiled bank raid:

- Verdicts of double murder and suicide were returned at the inquest a week later.
- Charles Kennedy, an Oxford University student whose studies had been interrupted by war service, was said to have been 'so considerate that he would not run over a rabbit'.
- Witnesses of an earlier bank raid, at Bristol, travelled up to Penrith to see the body of Kennedy in the mortuary but no more was heard of any possible involvement in the Bristol crime.

Violent death was not a frequent occurrence in the tranquil countryside of the Eden Valley and the dales of Northern Lakeland. While occasional killings caused shock and horror, there were no 'whodunit' murder mysteries or long, involved investigations. After they happened the finger of guilt pointed unerringly at an individual, although questions could surround the degree of intent and premeditation and, sometimes, the sanity of the suspect.

Our ardour was tested by harrowing tragedies, as when the telephone sounded in a police station. The woman caller was heard to say: 'I have killed my children. I have killed my children.' The bodies of babies, aged two years and two months, were found in a remote house in the Cumbrian countryside, both killed by their mother, a piteously depressed and distraught woman. Prosecuting counsel at her trial said: 'Murder is the intentional killing by a person of sound mind and understanding of another human being. . . .'

The woman gazing from the dock was obviously not 'of sound mind and understanding' and everybody in the Assize court – prosecution, defence and the judge – were agreed that the verdict must be 'guilty but insane'. She was detained 'until Her Majesty's pleasure be known'.

Life's uncertainty was brought home when murder struck. One of the respected residents of a small town, a pillar of society, took his wife an early-morning cup of tea but then, in an inexplicable change of mood, beat his partner to death. When a young reporter, Bill Mossop, came back with the story, Robert Burne challenged the identity of the murderer, temporarily unable to accept that a gentle, loving husband could have behaved so savagely. The poor soul was found 'unfit to plead'.

Trouble erupted in the Eden Valley village of Brough in November 1959 when Westmorland County Council workmen arrived to remove an illuminated sign which had been erected without planning consent. Garage owner Watson Sayer tried to foil the attempt by hiring a Shorthorn bull from a local farmer and using the animal as a deterrent.

Under arrest! The bull was removed from the garage forecourt by PC Eric Wilson.

There were other murders – a fatal stabbing in a village street, a crime of passion in which a husband killed his young wife, and a glimpse of big city gangland when a man was shot aboard a night express train – but violent death did not necessarily produce the most readable news stories.

My favourite stories invariably had the stamp of rarity or uniqueness – such as the tactics employed by an Eden Valley businessman to defy local authority almost 40 years ago.

There were five of us in the village of Brough on that never-to-be-forgotten morning in November 1959. My companions were Ken Nicholson, of the *Penrith Observer*; Harry Griffin, the Kendal representative of the *Lancashire Evening Post*; Dan Lees, a *Daily Express* reporter, and Penrith freelance photographer Eric Davidson.

Most of us had received the strident call the previous evening: 'If you want a good story, get yourself to Brough tomorrow.' At the other end of the telephone was a man who was no stranger to controversy, Watson E. Sayer, a local entrepreneur and go-getter, whose word was not be to ignored. 'Watty' was the epitome of the self-made man – a one-time farm worker who went to sea but returned to his native territory and, by initiative and sheer hard work, achieved much business success in quarrying, mining, transport and, in November 1959, catering.

What greeted us at Brough that day was a superbly stage-managed protest, the latest chapter in a long-running battle against officialdom.

The hub of the dispute was an illuminated sign, bearing the words 'Sayer's 24-Hour Garage and Café', which stood on the forecourt of a recently built garage-cum-café, 'Watty' Sayer's latest business venture. He had put up the sign without permission from the Westmorland planning authorities who demanded its removal. After three years of impasse, a date was arranged for the arrival of council workmen, with electricians, to take down the offending sign, because Mr. Sayer refused to do so himself. He said that it was essential if the business was to succeed, but the planners countered: 'This sign cannot be allowed to remain because, sooner or later, people will hold it up as a precedent. Such signs are too blatant for people passing through this district.'

Planners and workmen arrived at Brough to find a situation which might have come straight out of a Will Hay comedy film. Their path to the sign was barred by a formidable looking Shorthorn bull, tethered to the post and clearly not the type of impediment which office-bound officials were accustomed to coping with. It must be said, however, that, despite his initial surprise at the type of sentry, planning officer William Wark, who was in charge of the operation, dealt with the entire affair with aplomb and affability. He stayed remarkably cool and composed throughout the removal of the sign, although he no doubt hoped for swifter progress than the ensuing five hours of heated exchanges and obstructive tactics, spiced with a fair measure of hilarity.

'Watty' Sayer took centre stage, although the hero of the episode was surely Eric Wilson, the PC from the nearby village of Ravenstonedale, who stepped forward to lead away the bull, to the accompaniment of jeers and boos from workers and villagers, Enterprising journalists christened the animal 'Neon

Nonsense' and reckoned that its pedigree was probably 'by Confusion out of Town Planning'.

Despite PC Wilson's moment of glory, we had not seen the last of 'Neon Nonsense'. Penrith photographer Alec Fraser arrived late, having received an order for a picture from one of the daily papers, and sought a picture of the bull standing alongside the famous sign. Officialdom protested but 'Watty' Sayer said the man must have the picture he wanted and the animal was led back onto the forecourt for a brief encore.

With this and other hiatuses impeding progress, it was mid-afternoon before men with acetylene burners finally brought down the sign and by then it had achieved more publicity than its colourful owner could ever have hoped for.

Rare, perhaps unique, the story of 'Watty' Sayer's bull is only one illustration of how the air of uncertainty is keener in journalism than in most other professions. Sometimes the element of unpredictability can verge upon the terrifying, even life-threatening.

Photographer Eric Davidson, my companion on a mission to report on a big blasting operation, was lucky to return alive. The explosion, on Shap Fell, was intended to bring down 90,000 tons of high quality granite at the Wasdale Quarry, much of it for use in a new dock on the Manchester Ship Canal. As a safety measure, most of the quarry workers were evacuated to watch from the A6 road, some 700 yards from the quarry face. However, nobody raised any objection when

Planning officer William Wark called on PC Eric Wilson to remove the bull, so that demolition work could proceed. However, Mr Sayer insisted that the animal be brought back so that a photographer could get a picture when he arrived late! Mr Sayer is to the right of the bull in the bottom picture.

Eric chose a point closer to the action, lying on his stomach in a field between the main road and the quarry, with camera at the ready.

Although experts had been brought in to supervise, the blast went badly wrong, sending massive chunks of granite whirling through the air towards the roadway and the crowds of spectators. One veteran workman, who, with a companion, had not retreated as far as the rest, was killed, out of sight of onlookers. What they saw was the imminent threat to Eric Davidson who, as soaring stones rained down on the field where he lay, appeared to be transfixed in horror – although he still got his picture.

My story, headed 'Tragedy mars Shap's biggest blast', contained this extract: 'He (Eric Davidson) was in the act of taking them (pictures) in the field dividing the road from the quarry when a terrific boulder buried itself in the ground only a few feet from where he was lying. Its weight was estimated at 4½-5 tons. The crater measured roughly twelve feet across . . . Mr Davidson said, "I saw it whizzing in my direction but I did not know which way to run. It was a terrifying moment".'

It was not the only near-miss. Another chunk of stray granite travelled over 600 yards to strike a car which a holidaymaker had parked alongside the A6. Luckily, the man and his wife got out to watch the explosion a mere second or so before the whirling rock crashed through the windscreen and buried itself in the passenger's seat.

A week later, at the inquest on the dead workman, Eric Davidson's dramatic picture was produced as evidence of how the explosion had gone wrong. North Westmorland Coroner William Scorer said, 'When you try to calculate what is going to happen in a blast of this kind, there is no knowing what tricks Nature may have played in putting the rock together.'

Scrutiny focused on public rights of way in the 1950s. Where doubts occurred about claims that field walks existed, officials of the county council were called on to adjudicate and held inquiries in village halls.

Old romances were refreshed by ageing couples recalling their courting days, spent meandering together through fields and hedgerows. The memories provided richly nostalgic evidence that paths certainly existed when they were sweet sixteen. Landowners tended to fight such claims with vehemence and ingenuity. Some would allege that walkers were in their fields to poach rabbits, rather than through any love of rural strolls.

One local squire stole the show at one of the inquiries by pooh-poohing the romantic recollections of village pensioners. 'Yes,' he said disdainfully. 'There was a path but not for anybody. It was the bull trod for the exclusive use of the parish bull as it was moved from farm to farm, in and around the village.'

Of course, he added, there was no longer a parish bull to serve local cattle herds. So the only person entitled to use the path in more modern times was the man from the artificial insemination centre with his injecting equipment. His claim sounded 'a lot of bull' and villagers were told the path was still theirs to enjoy.

In 1957 I helped to report the last days of Lowther Castle, the stately residence a few miles south of Penrith. The final disintegration of the once-magnificent interior was about to begin, although it still presents a majestic appearance to the outside world, thanks to the preservation of the battlemented walls which form its handsome facade.

Before the demolition men moved in, the castle was opened to the public enabling about 6,000 Cumbrians to take a step back in time and get some impression of the great days when the castle was the home of the Earls of Lonsdale – a sombre pilgrimage into a colourful and lively past. It was a sad thought that so much of the beauty in architecture and decoration would soon be coming under the breaker's hammer.

Although the castle was chill and damp after many years of disuse, there was a lingering impression of the pomp and splendour which had surrounded illustrious hosts and celebrated guests in a more spacious age. From lofty halls and stately bedrooms, we moved 'below stairs' and saw mute reminders of the immense domestic organization which had been responsible for the cooking and cleaning, the sweeping and dusting, the carrying of fuel and food, the making of beds and the washing of dishes. One writer described it as 'a monument to domestic inconvenience'.

A showpiece among the faded grandeur was a famous stained glass window, facing down the main staircase, which was given to the 5th Earl of Lonsdale by the Emperor of Germany, Kaiser Wilhelm II, when he visited Lowther in 1895. At the demolition sale, a fortnight later, the window was sold for £50 to Prince Frederick of Prussia, the Kaiser's grandson.

Rarity of experience could be found in the most unexpected of places. After an Eden Valley farmer died in a tractor accident, Coroner William Scorer chose to hold the inquest in the kitchen of his farmhouse home, which gave the proceedings an ethos of Dickensian dignity and beauty, compared with the more usual setting of a courthouse or a village hall.

The coroner sat at the kitchen table, slowly writing down the quietly spoken evidence, but, otherwise, life went on as usual. Above the scratch of the pen and the gentle burr of voices, the dominant sounds were the placid, everyday sounds of the farmhouse – the solemn tick of the grandfather clock, the occasional crackle of coal from the black-leaded fireplace and the almost imperceptible creak of a rocking chair seating the dead man's mother, an elderly woman whose face showed no trace of the sadness she must have been feeling. The farm cat was fast asleep at her feet. A Hollywood film director could not have stage-managed a scene as moving as this one.

Outside, the sunshine highlighted the close-up radiance of roadside verges and hedgerows and, beyond, the great expanse of the Eden Valley stretched away for miles like a multi-coloured jigsaw puzzle of fields, trees, farmhouses and hamlets. I thought of the farmer who must have relished all this beauty, both indoors and outdoors, until death struck. Could he possibly find a paradise to equal this earthly one?

CHAPTER 15

Watershed in Time

Vanished times? How do you quantify them and determine that precise moment when older, more serene days gave way to relative modernity – to hustle and bustle, the 'rat race' – and former ways and lifestyles began to ebb away.

I would say that the new era began in earnest at precisely 12.28 p.m. on Thursday, 7th November 1968. Robert Brown, Joint Parliamentary Secretary to the Ministry of Transport, cut a ribbon, barricades were removed and the first traffic surged along the eight-mile section of the M6 motorway which bypasses Penrith. The town was to become a better place to live in, the politician predicted.

The transitional period had taken almost forty years of planning and pleading, years full of doubt, indecision and fear. The first scheme for a loop round Penrith, suggested in 1930, was never followed up because of a national financial crisis, but in 1953 a new call went out, this time from John Watson and Isaac Sim, two leading councillors. They described Penrith's traffic conditions as 'chaotic', especially during the Glasgow holiday when policemen struggled to keep vehicles moving. A survey was ordered to seek the views of drivers and decide on the priority to be given to a bypass. By 1953 the cost had risen to a million pounds.

Twelve more years were to pass before work actually began on the long-awaited relief road. On a sunny morning in early August, 1965, I accompanied photographer Alec Fraser when he motored out along the old Penrith-Ullswater road, near Skirsgill, to take pictures of county council workmen removing slices of turf and putting them in neat piles in a field between the road and the main London to Glasgow railway line. A bridge was to be built at this point to carry the railway over the route of the M6; the construction of the bridge was to start later in 1965 and work on the motorway itself in the following year. Watching the men at work and looking south over nearby fields, there was a sudden realization of the true cost of the bypass. Quite apart from unimaginable sums of money, Penrith was to pay for it in lush meadows, country walks, climbing trees, birds' nests, frolicsome rabbits and the quaintly named Horse Shoe pond (which children believed was bottomless!).

Penrith paid a heavy price, over and above the £10 million which the bypass cost by the time it was completed on 7th November 1968. Among the countless changes, none made a more emotional impact than the M6 on the countryside on the outskirts of town. Etched on my mind, as seen from my parents' old house at Skirsgill Gardens, is a landscape of fields dipping and rising in an unbroken sequence of pasture, woods and hedges and ranging away to the Ullswater hills

A significant picture in the post-war history of Penrith, taken in 1965. The removal of turf from a sloping field, on the western fringe of the town, was the first visible sign of the impending construction of the Penrith bypass section of the M6 (opened in 1968). The motorway and Junction 40 now dominate the scene but in 1965, cattle still grazed in the field beyond the road and children visited Horse Shoe pond on a field path to collect tadpoles and frog-spawn.

and the more distant grandeur of Saddleback. Immediate fields were places for impromptu cricket and football matches, for picking mushrooms and for the grazing of livestock, over which auction mart foreman Dick Turner cast a watchful eye. The predominant sounds were of bird song – the lark and the thrush, the curlew and the peewit.

Now the air throbs continuously with the sound of traffic from the M6, just two old fields away, although nowadays the intervening land bears no resemblance to the outlook of years long past and is full of houses, bungalows and a posh hotel. They cut through old memories of footpaths, childhood games, cross-country runs and lovers' strolls into the sunset.

There has been a blur of changes in Penrith, some for the better. Old-style grocery emporiums were among the victims of a more helter-skelter society,

Pictures taken on 7 November 1968 at the opening of Penrith bypass by Robert Brown, Joint Parliamentary Secretary to the Ministry of Transport. The official party arrives.

ousted by the less characterful – but decidedly cheaper – supermarkets. As a result, some shopping streets went into decline, through closures and empty windows, although there was compensation in the development of attractive shopping malls and the refurbishment of the market arcade.

Trends in evening entertainment cost the town some of its chummy pubs, the Horse and Farrier, the Mitre, the White Horse, the Fish and the Blue Bell. Drinking goes on but in the nightclubs, the sports and ex-servicemen's clubs – and at home, in front of the television. The Alhambra cinema has survived the TV era, with the aid of a number of weekly bingo sessions, but gone is the Regent where the double seats on the back row were much sought after by courting couples.

The auction mart moved out of town – to the other side of the motorway – and we no longer see the old-time bullock-wallopers driving livestock along the streets.

Law and order suffered through the extension of the M6 to Penrith and beyond. Once, if a house was burgled, suspicion immediately fell on one of the town's three established housebreakers. Detective work became markedly more toilsome when big city criminals flooded into the area along the motorway.

The wail of the old fire buzzer is no longer heard when somebody is in trouble, for Penrith has a more modern brigade stationed on the outskirts where grass

Crowds gather at Junction 40, the point where town traffic joins the M6.

once grew in meadows. Nearby are the health centre and a new hospital, successors to the individual surgeries of individual doctors, and to the cottage hospital built to mark Queen Victoria's diamond jubilee.

'Penrith will be a better place to live in,' said Robert Brown as he opened the bypass. Yes, in many ways his prediction has been accurate. The town centre has become quiet enough to shop in and to gossip in. Previously the traffic crawled in lengthy grinding queues, with heavy lorries delayed by the 'bottlenecks' in the main street.

Distinctive old properties – some would call them slums – were swept away to make room for an inner ring road which never came to fruition. They have been replaced by new housing estates, on which admirable new schools have been developed. You don't evaluate a town by looking at the state of its roads or the range of its shops and services. Penrith has an enduring quality as a caring town, thanks to voluntary organizations which serve all kinds of needs. Pick up any issue of the *Herald* and you will read of the activities and ambitions of the old people's welfare council, the hospital 'friends', the museum 'friends', the talking newspaper, carers' groups, transport volunteers, the civic society, Citizen's Advice Bureau, the stroke club, the Rotary Club, Inner Wheel and a range of other worthy bodies.

The old-time closeness may have faded somewhat as the town grew but it is still small enough to be good natured and gossipy. A walk through the streets is usually punctuated with first-name greetings and short chats with old acquaintances. From time to time we hear expressions of concern about the

The white tape flutters to the ground as the bypass is opened.

deterioration of life in the countryside, resulting from declines in farming and the arrival of 'townies' in rural havens. Some villages have suffered through the closure of pubs, shops, post offices and schools, but others have benefited from developments made possible by their proximity to the M6, without losing their essential character. Orton has a small chocolate factory in the former school, for instance. Most villages still display strong evidence of community spirit and pride in their surroundings. Many – for example, Askham, Maulds Meaburn, Kirkoswald, Warcop, Winton, Garrigill and Mungrisdale – are so strikingly beautiful that they would grace the lid of any chocolate box.

What then of the *Herald* in the years of change – and in the future?

Gone are the reporters' pushbikes as a means of getting to news assignments. Gone, too, the handwritten and typed copy, for the computer is king and editorial and advertising offices are full of word processor keyboards.

It was my colleague Frank Shaw who, during his tenure as editor, supervised the change-over, introducing, stage by stage, technological aids to achieve swifter production.

A final reminder of a past age of production was removed in 1988 by the departure of 'Intertype No. 36522, Model C', the last of the trusty Linotypes. The distinctive clanking and the pungent smell of these typesetting machines were essential to the operation — the pride of the printing works. Manned by genial men in leather aprons, they spat out the news in lines of hot lead.

Alas for the noble Linotype, it could not match the microchip which revolutionized newspaper production. Computerized setting ousted the old

Construction of the M6 motorway through Cumbria involved a major pipe-laying operation.

Crowds lined the street in Middlegate, Penrith, in June 1962 to watch the famous Dagenham Girl Pipers march past on the occasion of the opening of the Fine Fare supermarket.

machines and ended the din of the printing works. Initially, the silence seemed unreal; the works could have been a Victorian drawing room.

Newspapermen of the future will never know the buzz of energy and atmosphere which 'Linos' gave the premises. On visits to the works, schoolchildren were given pieces of lead bearing their names, by way of souvenirs. Production of the paper without these reliable, if noisy, machines seemed unthinkable at one time.

And what of the future of the local paper?

However rose-tinted or however gloomy our vision of the future, people in small towns and villages will always want to know what is happening all around them and, in particular, the deeds and misdeeds, the feats and the failings of their friends and neighbours. News and information already flow into our homes, available at the touch of a button, via radio, television or a fax machine. The predictions are that technological advances are such that computers will soon be able to tell us all the news and enable us to buy goods from distant shopping malls without leaving the house.

But weekly newspapers of character and a decent code of behaviour, like the

A street-long load. Devonshire Street, on the main road through Penrith, is almost filled by a huge steel cylinder, en route from Stockton-on-Tees to the British Petroleum Company's refinery at Grangemouth. The driver is about to negotiate the 'Narrows'; the town's notorious bottleneck. Such monsters now travel along the M6.

Herald, still have a role. They are an integral part of the way of life of smaller communities and vital to the democratic system, providing liaison between public bodies and the people who elect them, and championing causes of importance.

More than that, of course, the *Herald* is genuinely loved by many of its readers. No, 'love' is not too strong a word to use, for the paper has become an intrinsic part of people's lives and its arrival is looked forward to every Saturday morning, in the way that a rendezvous with an old friend is awaited eagerly. Sir John Betjeman once wrote: 'While the nationals deal with remote happenings and remote people, the local paper presents the news of the things and the people we all know. The news is the real news; it comes from Britain's heart. It is never quoted by *Pravda*, nor by the *New York Times*, but the weekly local newspaper is England.'

Local newspapers are seldom sensational, nor do they seize on news which hurts, rather than pleases, and they strive to be entirely accurate. The editor of the local paper cannot afford to be anything else because he has to live with the people long after the paper comes out.

Every column of the local paper is read and believed – every one of the advertisements, as well as reports ranging from council debates and court hearings to chapel anniversaries and WI meetings, complete with competition winners and lists of those who helped with serving refreshments and the washing-up.

Some things are irreplaceable because of their uniqueness and they include newspapers like the *Herald* as purveyors of news, pictures and advertisements in vast areas containing more sheep than men!

CHAPTER 16

The Survivor

The newspaper tradition in the Cumbrian town of Penrith is long and strong.

The *Cumberland and Westmorland Herald*, now aged 136, is the sole survivor of three papers which were founded within six years of each other – the *Cumberland and Westmorland Advertiser* (in 1855) and the *Herald* and the *Penrith Observer* (both 1860).

Competition for circulation and advertising was fierce. The three papers also went through revolutionary mechanical changes because of the development of the first typesetting machine by Linotype, an invention which ended the laborious task of setting type by hand, with compositors picking up the letters one at a time.

The *Advertiser* was the first victim of the town's newspaper war. A drop in circulation in the 1890s led to a change of title to the *Penrith Times* and a transfer of publication from Tuesday (market day) to Saturday, in direct competition with the *Herald*. The *Penrith Times* ceased publication in 1901.

Rivalry can be a potent force in keeping newspapermen on their toes. The *Penrith Observer* was such a spur but, generally, a friendly rival and there was a degree of collaboration with the *Herald* in the sharing of transport. Sadly, publication of the *Observer* ended in 1968.

The founder-editor of the *Herald* in 1860 was a young man named Thomas Hodgson who had come to the town from Barnard Castle some years before, originally to work for the *Advertiser*. The *Herald* was under his proprietorship until the 1890s when a company was set up.

Remarkably, the paper has had only seven editors in its 136 years – Thomas Hodgson, Tom Sarginson, Robert Irving, George Hobley, Frank Shaw, John Hurst and Colin Maughan. The last six all worked as *Herald* reporters before succeeding to the editorship. So did Bill Mossop, now the managing director. There was pride in 1993 when the paper received a top environmental award in recognition of its support during campaigns to prevent pollution in the Cumbrian countryside. The anti-litter theme earned the *Herald* one of the Queen Mother's birthday awards for environmental improvement, made by the Tidy Britain Group and presented in a London hotel. But the most desirable form of recognition for any newspaper is that from its readers, reflected in circulation figures. The *Herald* set a record of 20,176 in 1990 and, although the total has fallen slightly, almost 20,000 copies go out from Penrith each week – some bound for loyal readers on the other side of the world.

At the heart of **Herald** *country. In the foreground is the town of Penrith where the newspaper has been published for 136 years; in the distance are the fells around Ullswater. Since this picture was taken, the landscape has been altered considerably by the construction of the M6 and later developments on the far side of town, including housing, an auction mart and a hotel.*

More of the **Herald** *country, this time the Tebay Gorge in the days before the M6 was extended northwards into what is now Cumbria; then the old county of Westmorland. The motorway now sweeps across this countryside and is the main north–south route for thousands of heavy-goods vehicles every day.*

On 2 January 1945 John Hurst was a nervous newcomer to the reporting staff of the
Cumberland and Westmorland Herald. *On 2 January 1995 he was almost as nervous when*
he walked into the printing works to find he was guest of honour at a champagne party being
given to directors and colleagues in the editorial, printing and advertising departments, in
recognition of his fifty years with the paper. He retired from the editorship in May 1995 and
still writes a weekly column for the Herald. *Front row, (left to right): Bill Mossop (managing*
director), George Veitch (director), John Hurst (editor/director), Frank Shaw (director and
former editor), Lindsay Kidd (chairman of directors) and Brian Spurrett (advertising
manager).

Acknowledgements

The author owes a debt of gratitude to Mrs Nancy Stonehouse for her invaluable help in preparing the manuscript and in other ways.

The majority of the pictures were taken, mainly in the 1950s and 1960s, by Robert Armstrong, Eric Davidson and Alec Fraser, plus one by John T. Hall. They are reproduced by permission of Mrs Hilary Armstrong, Alec Fraser, John T. Hall and the *Cumberland and Westmorland Herald Limited*. Pictures were loaned by Geoffrey Harrington and Roland Kirkbride.

Frederick C. Wilson, the photographer serving the *Herald* at the time of writing, gave much help in producing prints from old negatives. Mrs Evelyn Glasson (formerly Rae) kindly passed on some of her recollections of the 1950s.

General Index

Index of Illustrations